The Volunteer

The Volunteer

*A Personal Toolkit
for the
Dedicated Volunteer*

Doug Fagerstrom

BMH Books
www.bmhbooks.com
Winona Lake, IN 46590

The Volunteer: A Personal Toolkit for the Dedicated Volunteer

Copyright ©2009 by Douglas Fagerstrom

ISBN: 978-0-88469-074-0
RELIGION / Christian Ministry / General.
Printed in the United States of America

Published by BMH Books
BMH Books, P.O. Box 544, Winona Lake, IN 46590 USA
www.bmhbooks.com

Dedication

To my "Super Volunteer" Dad

Who, in his late 80s, teaches a Bible study in his retirement
community, leads singing at a nursing home worship service,
takes two blind men shopping once a week, leads worship and has
been the co-host in his Sunday School class, provided care for my
mom, afflicted with Alzheimer's disease (died December 1, 2008),
and is still considered the number one volunteer to
the support staff at mom's care facility.

"A senior saint, called by God to do the work of the ministry."
Ephesians 4:12

Table of Contents

Foreword

"Will anyone volunteer…?" is a familiar sound in churches and charitable organizations all over the globe. Usually an extended, awkward silence makes everyone a little unsettled… particularly if the one asking for volunteers keeps looking at you. Finally, often just to break the deadlock, someone raises his hand and the deed is done. He is now a "volunteer."

What's next? Show up for the assignment and hopefully get a thank you now and then? Well, there has to be more to it than that. And there is. But, unfortunately, while volunteers are usually the most important group in a lot of organizations, they remain the most under trained and under recognized group in the club.

When was the last time you saw a book on being a great volunteer? The list of books on leadership and management, written to help the well-paid professionals, is long. But, if you had asked me last month to recommend a book on volunteerism I would have drawn a blank. No longer. Thankfully, we now have a great read on what it means to navigate life when your title is "volunteer."

My friend Doug Fagerstrom has made a long overdue contribution to every organization that rides the wave of its voluntary work force. The full-timers should read this to understand the frustrations and dilemmas of being a non-paid partner. And, obviously, if you want to thrive in and enjoy volunteering, then this is just the book for you.

I've worked in lots of organizations where volunteers were key to the success of the mission. They are my heroes. And, if you doubt the importance of being a volunteer, think of what twelve volunteers pulled off when they raised their hands to follow Jesus!

Dr. Joseph M Stowell III
President, Cornerstone University

Preface

The Volunteer is not a book that talks *about* volunteers. This book is a conversation *with* you, the volunteer. It is *written to* volunteer women and men wherever you serve.

The plain vanilla definition of a volunteer is frequently debated. The Merriam-Webster Dictionary defines a volunteers as "a person who voluntarily undertakes or expresses a willingness to undertake a service: one who enters into military service voluntarily" or "one who renders a service or takes part in a transaction while having no legal concern or interest." Some say a volunteer is someone who performs or offers to perform service out of his or her own free will, without payment, usually in support of a non-profit organization, mission-based initiative, or community. (See the current popular definition in the inset box quoting Wikipedia.com, Volunteer.) That description does not compel me to raise my hand to commit my time and energy the next time a volunteer is requested from the leader on the platform. There has to be more.

> ## What is a Volunteer?
>
> A volunteer is someone who works for free for a community for the benefit of natural environment primarily because he or she chooses to do so. The word comes from Latin, and can be translated as "will" (as in doing something out of one's own free will). Many serve through a non-profit organization—sometimes referred to as formal volunteering, but a significant number also serve less formally, either individually or as part of a group (Wikipedia).

Actually, there is more. Every believer should be a volunteer in Christian ministry. Every believer has at least one God-given gift. Every believer has a responsibility before God and the community of believers to use that gift. *As volunteers, we serve Jesus Christ and others with our God-given gifts and skills without any consideration of what*

i

we will get in return. While there are great rewards and marvelous returns for serving God and others, that is not our motive to serve.

Caleb is one of my quiet heroes in the Bible. He served with wholehearted devotion. His initial work was voluntary. He signed up for a tough task. For his entire life he was faithful and committed not to waiver from the work God had assigned. Throughout *The Volunteer* I hope you see the underlying theme of wholehearted devotion and service to God and others. Volunteerism is not just about our time and talents. It is about giving every area of our heart, mind, soul, and strength. Don't hold back. Give back everything God has given you.

Volunteering in the church and other Christ-centered ministries can be one of the most fulfilling, rewarding, and significant experiences in your life. In fact, it should be most meaningful and contagious. At the end of the day, volunteering is personal engagement in the work of God, and, ultimately, results in transformed lives. The final outcome will be measured only in eternity, but the payback now and later can be enormous.

So, sometime this week, somewhere in God's kingdom, with a variety of capacities, and a multitude of personal resources and giftedness, you and I will be volunteers. Maybe it will be at a church, or school, or local clinic, helping a friend or neighbor, agreeing to support a meaningful mission in the community or within the context of our workplace. It is embedded in our North American culture to give of our time, treasure, and talents. Volunteers are everywhere. You will find them in the Boy Scouts, Girl Scouts, Big Brother/Big Sister program, relief and crisis agencies, hospitals, schools, and in our churches. We cannot escape the opportunities. Volunteerism is here to stay.

Loving God by loving others and *serving God by serving others* are the motivational mantras. That is what being a volunteer is really all about. It is not about feeding an ego, finding a social place to be applauded, or exercising authority and control over others. The Christian volunteer is motivated and compelled by God's love for us, which, when appropriated, causes us to love others. My wife Donna says it well, "I serve in my church out of obedience to Christ and God's calling in my life." Doing God's work God's way is a great joy.

When done for God's glory, every volunteer action can be marked by love, grace, and mercy.

"Sacrifice" is an amazingly welcomed word in a godly volunteer's vocabulary. Giving of one's self becomes generous and automatic. It is not contrived or forced. Paul the apostle said,

> If I give all I possess to the poor and surrender my body to the flames, but have not love, I gain nothing (1 Corinthians 13:3).

> Your attitude should be the same as that of Christ Jesus: Who, being in very nature God, did not consider equality with God something to be grasped, but made himself nothing, taking the very nature of a servant, being made in human likeness. And being found in appearance as a man, he humbled himself and became obedient to death—even death on a cross! (Philippians 2:5-8).

> What is more, I consider everything a loss compared to the surpassing greatness of knowing Christ Jesus my Lord, for whose sake I have lost all things. I consider them rubbish, that I may gain Christ (Philippians 3:8).

> Though I am free and belong to no man, I make myself a slave to everyone, to win as many as possible (1 Corinthians 9:19).

When I walk into my local Starbucks, I hear, "Good morning, how may I *serve* you?" They've got the right idea. So much more should the Christian volunteer get it right, that of humble loving service to one another. I believe we can raise the old volunteer standards a notch or two. This book might help you do just that.

The Volunteer will encourage, energize, and equip you with the basics. It will challenge you to move beyond where you are today. In this book you, the volunteer, will learn to create realistic expectations, ask the right questions within your service context, become more engaged in ministry, discover more of what God has for you, and find greater purpose and joy in serving Jesus and others. It is written to you, the volunteer, but it also serves as a voice to your leaders, as they eavesdrop on our conversation. It can become the catalyst for discussion among other volunteers or the church staff. It might also be used as the outline for a volunteer retreat or training program.

Quotations, insights, and tabulations from a survey of more than 100 volunteers are included in *The Volunteer*. The survey is found in Appendix 1. Volunteers were given the survey at random in more than 20 different social and ministry contexts. I am confident that more than 50 different ministries are represented in the unbiased, though unscientific, survey. The survey provides real responses from real volunteers.

Read this book with an open heart. Refer back to it time and again when you need a tool for your ministry toolkit. Read with great expectations of what God can do. When you have finished reading, pass your newly found energy and insights on to others. Don't wait for an invitation. Take the initiative to create ministry with others. They and you will be glad you did.

There is no question; you are God's servant in His kingdom! So am I! Let's serve wholeheartedly!

Rejoicing and volunteering with you,
Doug Fagerstrom

Introduction

You Are Called by God to Minister to People

Volunteers are chosen, gifted, and called by God.
(Pastor Bill Rudd, Calvary Church, Fruitport, Michigan)

"God called me to volunteer as a fourth grade Sunday School teacher 32 years ago. I can't imagine doing anything more fulfilling and meaningful. What a joy to know scores of boys and girls from our little church who are now serving the Lord Jesus all over the world."
("Mrs. Ann")

And you will be called priests of the LORD,
you will be named ministers of our God.
(Isaiah 61:6)

But you are a chosen people, a royal priesthood, a holy nation, a people belonging to God, that you may declare the praises of him who called you out of darkness into his wonderful light.
(1 Peter 2:9)

It was just before the Passover Feast. Jesus knew that the time had come for him to leave this world and go to the Father. Having loved his own who were in the world, he now showed them the full extent of his love…Jesus knew that the Father had put all things under his power, and that he had come from God and was returning to God; so he got up from the meal, took off his outer clothing, and wrapped a towel around his waist. After that, he poured water into a basin and began to wash his disciples' feet, drying them with the towel that was wrapped around him.
(John 13:1, 3-5)

Introduction

As a new pastor at Calvary Church, it was my first weekend with our single adult ministry leadership team. It was a wonderful and whimsical time of getting acquainted with people my wife and I had never met before. They were volunteers, every one of them. I was the only person who received a paycheck from the church.

During our initial devotional time, the leader of the group, his name is also Doug, shared the intimate story of Jesus and His disciples from John 13, when Jesus washes His disciples' feet. While the story teaches a deep spiritual truth about Jesus as our high priest and His cleansing role soon anticipated on the cross, it also paints a powerful picture of our savior, the humble servant. Doug did very well sharing the story, reminding everyone that we are also servants to one another.

I was really enjoying our time of devotions with my new ministry team, until Doug invited me to take off my shoes and socks. I felt

---

The Old Testament Servant

Moses, David, and the prophets of God are the best known servants of the Lord in the Old Testament (Deut. 34:5; 2 Sam. 7:5; Isa. 20:3; Amos 3:7). Their primary characteristic was obedience to God in the face of adversity and the unknown. While they argued with God and sometimes took matters into their own hands, they remained faithful to God and followed the leading of God's spirit.

In Isaiah 42, the servant of the LORD (Jehovah) is:
>   *Verse 1:*   Called by God, Holy Spirit empowered with strength and godly justice.
>   *Verse 2:*   Gentle and meek
>   *Verse 3:*   Sensitive and faithful
>   *Verse 4:*   Persevering to the end.

The OT paints a picture of the servant with unbridled obedience to God and His Word. There is an undeniable walk of faith. Selfishness is nearly non-existent. The cares and concerns of others supersede personal agendas.

God's servant loves God, His Word, and His people.

rather uncomfortable, crooked toenails and all. Obviously, I could not refuse his humble request as he imitated Jesus by taking a bowl of water, a hand towel, and washed my feet. I heard only water cascading into the plastic bowl and a few sniffles from other volunteers in the soft silence of the moment.

As the volunteer leader of the single adult ministry, Doug understood that to mean, *I am servant of all.* He got it right for all of us. Three years later I hired him as a full-time ministry staff leader. Three years after joining our staff, Doug went on to become the senior pastor of a fast-growing church in the Chicago area. He continues his ministry as a servant of Christ, called of God. He still understands the role of servant.

What Doug did was unforgettable. What Jesus did is even more unbelievable. As God calls each of us to be his children, he invites us to serve him with all our heart, soul, mind, and strength. That pretty much takes care of all that we are and have. What a calling! What a privilege! In the Old Testament, the spy Caleb is known best for one thing, He followed and served God *wholeheartedly* (Joshua 14:6-14).

We Are Children of God.

Wouldn't it be awesome if the next time we answered the phone, it were God on the other end calling us? Well, He has called, not by phone, but by His gospel message extended to each of us. The creator God has initiated a call to every one of His sons and daughters. What an amazing calling. It is that godly initiative and divine invitation that lead us to privilege and responsibility within God's kingdom, family, and household of faith.

Paul urges the believers in the metropolitan city of Ephesus, "Live a life worthy of the calling you have received" (Ephesians 4:1). This was not some mystical call. It was a real call of God in their lives. They were now called Christians. They had just been adopted by God into His forever family (Ephesians 1:5). *They* belonged to Him. *We* belong to Him as believers in Christ. We have been bought with a price (1 Corinthians 6:20), therefore we are to honor and glorify God with our very lives as servants of Christ, serving one another.

As children, we learned at an early age to identify our parents or guardians apart from all other authority figures in our lives. We bore their name, the name of our family of origin or the name of our adopted family. We knew to whom we belonged. With that came certain unalienable rights and privileges. If we were good children, we enjoyed the privileges. If we were disobedient, we lost some privileges.

Living as worthy children is our privilege. It honors God. It enhances the lives of those around us. What does it mean to live worthy? The idea of worth is basically the idea of value. It does not take long to determine what is valuable in our lives and what has little to no value. We then make a series of choices, often choosing what is perceived as valuable. That is living a worthy life. The Christ-centered volunteer has high values right from the Bible.

As a child of God, as a volunteer in my church, I can make choices. I can choose what is of value or what is not. I can use my gifts from God or not use my gifts. I can choose to demonstrate the fruit of the spirit (Galatians 5:22-23), or I can choose to demonstrate the fruit of the culture around me. When I make those choices (and many more) I am demonstrating what is valuable, and I am determining the value of my calling as a child of the living God. Here are a *few* biblical values to consider.

- Reading and studying the Bible
- Creating a life of worship and celebration of God with others.
- Developing a lifestyle of knowing, caring, and praying for others.
- Faithfully giving a certain amount of my time and resources to this ministry.
- Designing to love, build up, encourage, comfort, and care for one another.

That is only a partial list of activities and intentions that are valuable to God for my life. Once I make those choices that reflect godly values, I am in the right place for serving God and others. Making lesser choices prepares me only to serve myself.

We Are Servants of Christ.

That is what we are. Make no mistake about it. Several times in the Bible we see Jesus, the servant (Matthew 12:18; Philippians 2:7) and Paul, the servant of Christ (Acts 26:16). Isn't it marvelous that the title God chose for his Son is reserved for us: servant!

In his parables Jesus taught the value of servanthood. He said:

"The greatest among you will be your *servant*" (Matthew 23:11, emphasis added).

Who then is the faithful and wise *servant*, whom the master has put in charge of the servants in his household to give them their food at the proper time? (Matthew 24:45, emphasis added).

His master replied, "Well done, good and faithful *servant*! You have been faithful with a few things; I will put you in charge of many things. Come and share your master's happiness!" (Matthew 25:23, emphasis added).

The New Testament Servant

Jesus sets the standard for servant in the New Testament. He came as a servant, giving up the glory and rights of His deity (Phil. 2:6-8). Yet as human and divine, He came to serve, not be served, but to lovingly give His life for the ungodly (Mark 10:45). Jesus willingly goes beyond the picture of any servant, which includes unbearable suffering (Luke 18:32). He volunteers to go to the cross out of obedience to God.

Jesus has no value in positions (Mark 10:25f) or in material possession (Luke 9:58). As a servant, Jesus blesses others (Acts 3:26), is anointed to preach good news, heals the sick, and with compassion removes the bondage in people's lives (Luke 4:18f), without sinning (1 Peter 2:22).

Jesus raises the standard of volunteer servant and invites us to follow Him (1 Peter 2:21f) without hesitation. Paul makes that commitment (1 Corinthians 11:1) and urges each of us to do the same.

The New Testament picture of a volunteer servant? Jesus!

On a much more personal level, Jesus taught His disciples the principles of servanthood.

Sitting down, Jesus called the Twelve and said, "If anyone wants to be first, he must be the very last, and the *servant* of all" (Mark 9:35, emphasis added).

Whoever serves me must follow me; and where I am, my *servant* also will be. My Father will honor the one who serves me (John 12:26, emphasis added).

The apostle Paul does not skip a beat teaching the role of the servant.

21 Ways to Be a Servant
(The "One Anothers")

1.	Love	1 John 3:11
2.	Serve	Galatians 5:13
3.	Care	1 Corinthians 12:25
4.	Bear	Galatians 6:2
5.	Pray	James 5:16
6.	Honor	Romans 12:10
7.	Devote	Romans 12:10
8.	Stimulate	Hebrews 10:24
9.	Encourage	Hebrews 10:25
10.	Comfort	2 Corinthians 1:4
11.	Persevere	Ephesians 4:2
12.	Confess	James 5:16
13.	Forgive	Ephesians 4:32
14.	Be Kind	Ephesians 4:32
15.	Be Tender	Ephesians 4:32
16.	Be Humble	1 Peter 5:5
17.	Judge not	Romans 14:13
18.	Submit	Ephesians 5:21
19.	Be at Peace	Mark 9:50
20.	Unify	Ephesians 4:3
21.	Welcome	Romans 16:16

"And the Lord's *servant* must not quarrel; instead, he must be kind to everyone, able to teach, not resentful" (2 Timothy 2:24).

A brief profile and characteristics of a servant of Christ are enumerated in the above verses from the Bible. Servants are not quarrelsome; instead they are kind. They are able to teach others spiritual truth by their very lives as followers of Jesus. Servants are more concerned about following Jesus, not who is following them. Being first is not important. There are marvelous rewards, even though rewards are not the motive. Others see wisdom and faithfulness as twin giants in the life of the servant. A friend of mine, who volunteers in his church, has these words written in large letters on a wall in his house, "Believer or Follower of Jesus?"

Lesser-known disciples of Christ (Epaphras and Tychicus) were endeared partners with Paul in ministry. Note in the following verses the phrase "faithful minister," which characterizes, in part, their briefly written resumes of ministry and service.

> You learned it from Epaphras, our dear *fellow servant*, who is a *faithful minister* of Christ on our behalf (Colossians 1:7, emphasis added).

> Tychicus will tell you all the news about me. He is a *dear brother,* a *faithful minister* and *fellow servant* in the Lord (Colossians 4:7, emphasis added).

The writer of Hebrews comments, *Moses was* faithful *as a servant in all God's house* (Hebrews 3:2). In the following verses, the patriarchs of the church and an angel of the Lord could have commanded a title of honor and prestige, but they chose to use the title God gave them, *servant.*

- Simon Peter, a *servant* and apostle of Jesus Christ (2 Peter 1:1).
- James, *a servant* of God and of the Lord Jesus Christ (James 1:1).
- Jude, *a servant* of Jesus Christ and a brother of James, to those who have been called, who are loved by God the Father and kept by Jesus Christ (Jude 1).
- At this I fell at [an angel of God's] feet to worship him. But he said to me, "Do not do it! I am a *fellow servant* with you and with your brothers who hold to the testimony of Jesus. Worship God!" (Revelation 19:10).

I love the association, a *fellow servant with you and your brothers.* It is here we are connected as servants alongside God's special angelic agent and our eternal brothers and sisters in Christ. What a community! We are in this together. What a comfort!

God identifies His ministers, His agents of grace, as servants, including His Son, Jesus. And again, that is what we are, servants who imitate Jesus. Maybe the best way to understand the full impact of this biblical identity is to understand what we are not. As volunteers:

- We are not concerned about being in the lead, even though we may have a role of leadership.
- We are not always upfront for all to see, although we may have to be a point person within the community of volunteers.
- We are not always exonerated and applauded for our efforts, though there may be occasional recognition for a job well done.
- We are not looking for reward.
- We are not seeking advancement.

Servant-volunteers are concerned about being faithful ministers of the good news God has entrusted to us. We are agents of hope, peace, love, and joy. We do just that with kindness, tenderness, patience, and goodness. We desire to embrace, not push away. We hope for the best with no record of wrongs. We seek first God's kingdom, not our own kingdom or membership in another's.

I confess there were moments that I wanted to title this book, *The Servant.* Maybe you can call it that for me.

We Are Anointed.

The apostle John writes a letter from his pastoral ministry in Ephesus to the believers in his church and the surrounding areas within Asia. In his first of three pastoral letters he addresses the Christians in the churches as "Dear children" (1 John 2:18) and then makes a powerful statement, "But you have an anointing from the Holy One, and all of you know the truth" (v. 20). I believe that is one of the most significant declarations directed toward believers in the New Testament.

This anointing is not reserved for a few clergy members. It characterizes the empowerment of the Holy Spirit on those who are the forgiven "children" within Christ's body, the church (1 John 1:3;

Discovering Your Ministry
(more detail in chapter 7)

A simple formula can be a part of finding the place and role that God has designed for you.

Passion + Gift(s) + Arena = Ministry

"Passion" refers to the people whom God has called you to serve. Question: Who or what people group (youth, children, adults, etc.) do you love and think about the most?

"Gift(s)" refer to the spiritual gifts given by God.

"Arena" refers to your comfort and connection zone. Question: In what context do you best communicate and relate to people? One on one, in small groups, or large group settings?

2:1, 7-9, 12-13, 18, 28). The author does not select a few members within the church to remind them of this work of the Spirit. John is reminding all believers that we receive the Holy Spirit when we are adopted into God's family as His forever children. (Read Ephesians 1:5 and 13.) Volunteers can be anointed by God.

So, what does it mean to be "anointed" by God? The word anointed actually means "to assign a person to a special task, implying a giving of power by God to accomplish the task" (*Greek-English Reader's Lexicon of the New Testament*). God empowers believers with special gifts along with a special assignment. God not only endorses each believer's role, but He also grants the ability to perform that role. God does not leave us alone to figure out what and how we are going to do this thing called ministry.

Within the context of the community of believers it is our joy to discover that job from God and appropriate the tools He has for us to do His work. The rest is the thrill and joy of being obedient to God. The results are, again, eternal, or may I say, "out of this world."

Anointing has a very close relationship to the work of God's Holy Spirit in our lives. God chooses to become very intimate, not only in our salvation, but in our role of serving Him. "Now it is God who makes both us and you stand firm in Christ. He *anointed* us, set his

The Priesthood of Every Believer

The basic idea of the priesthood is that of mediator. Priests in the Old Testament mediated between God and the people of God for every need in life, both physical and spiritual.

After his atoning death and resurrection, Jesus became our perfect High Priest (Hebrews 4:14-16). He now sits on the throne of grace in heaven as our intercessory mediator, advocate, and counselor (1 John 2:1).

In 1 Peter, God calls us a "royal priesthood." That means we are royally united with Christ as He chose and adopted us and gave each of us a priestly role of prayer for one another, worship to God, and ministry to those in special need. In that we are all priests in God's new kingdom, we share this role together in corporate unity and responsibility.

seal of ownership on us, and put his Spirit in our *hearts* as a deposit, guaranteeing what is to come"(2 Corinthians 1:21, 22, emphasis added). You can't get much more personal than that. Anointing begins by God declaring that we belong to Him as we carry His name. (Remember the first few paragraphs in this chapter?) There is also a sense of future hope and glory in this verse, "guaranteeing what is to come." God is not only personal, but motivational.

Note the source in the above verses, "*He* anointed us." God makes it clear that we do not anoint each other for ministry. As fellow believers we have the joy of affirming and recognizing the Spirit's anointing in each other. Paul and John remind believers in Christ, we are *all* anointed by God. Now, that is something worth celebrating. And this anointing is not for a moment in time, but a gift of the Spirit that remains: "As for you, the anointing you received from him remains in you" (1 John 2:27a).

Jesus Christ was anointed by the Holy Spirit. Luke mentions how Jesus testifies of Himself, "The Spirit of the Lord is on me, because he has *anointed* me to preach good news to the poor" (Luke 4:18). Luke goes on in the book of Acts, "God *anointed* Jesus of Nazareth with the Holy Spirit and power, and how he went around doing good"

(Acts 10:38). Jesus Christ is anointed as our high priest (Hebrews 5:10). Now, he anoints us as priests to serve one another.

"But you are a chosen people, a royal priesthood, a holy nation, a people belonging to God, that you may declare the praises of him who called you out of darkness into his wonderful light" (1 Peter 2:9, see verse 5).

God's anointing us as a royal priesthood is closely linked to the teaching and guiding role of God's Spirit in the life of the believer (John 16:12-15). And this anointing carries us into future ministry to proclaim good news and do good, just as Jesus did. Is this not the most powerful work of God in the life of the volunteer who desires to serve Christ and His bride, the church?

We Are "The Church."

Together, that is what we are. The New Testament word for church is *ecclesia*. It simply means, "the called out ones of God." Indeed, we have been called out of a depressing world of darkness into a marvelous kingdom of light (Ephesians 5:8f). The Bible reminds us that we need to raise high the true light, Jesus, for all to see (John 8:12; Luke 8:16; 11:33). It is our privilege to let the world know who is the Light (Matthew 5:14, 15). Individually, that makes us lampstands. Together, we become a glorious candelabra.

We have already discussed that Christ followers (volunteers in the church) are His adopted children, servants, and God's anointed priests. Beyond that, there are numerous metaphors that help us understand what we are to look like as the church of Jesus Christ. First of all, Jesus is the head (Colossians 1:18). That is non-negotiable. We are illustrated in the Bible as branches, building blocks, a bride, body parts, family members, and sheep in God's pasture. The following verses would make a great Bible study for a group of volunteers. Read the verses and discuss the various connections to Christ and the responsibility each of us carries as a member of Jesus' church.

Texts	Role of God	Our Role as Volunteers
John 15:1-17	The True Vine	Branches that bear good fruit
Ephesians 2:14-22; 1 Peter 2:4-8	The Cornerstone	Building blocks holding up one another as a holy priesthood
Ephesians 5:22-29	The Bridegroom	Bride, faithful, loving, and submitted
Ephesians 4:16; 5:30; 1 Corinthians 12:12-31	The Head	Body parts, used to serve one another
Ephesians 3:14-4:16; 5:1; Galatians 6:10	The Father	Children, growing, maturing, and committed
John 10:1-21	The Shepherd	Sheep who follow, listen, and rest.

As volunteers in God's kingdom, we are joined together. Yet, we all have a job to do. We are to love, honor, and support each other. (See the sidebar: "21 Ways to Be a Servant." p. 6) These are not options. God desires that we volunteer and serve as one, a single unit, an army of many. We are in this together, forever. In the church we sing three love songs—one for God, one for each other, and the third for those Christ died for (John 3:16), those we will lovingly introduce to Christ and His family.

Questions to Ask Another Volunteer Ministry
Identify another respected volunteer ministry and ask the following questions.

- What special thing do you do to encourage volunteers?
- How do you train volunteers?
- How do volunteers participate in ministry decisions?
- How do you communicate to volunteers?
- How do volunteers initiate their own ministries?
- What expectations do you have of volunteers?
- What can volunteers expect from you?

Press On! Keep on Keeping On! Persevere! This is a message we don't often hear in a time when "I Quit" sounds so good. James chapter 1 reminds us that perseverance comes out of tough times, yet serves to develop maturity in our lives and ministries. Paul encourages believers to forget what is behind and press on ahead toward what God has called us heavenward for (Philippians 3:13).

The church of Jesus Christ needs you to persevere. Other discouraged volunteers and servants of Jesus need you to persevere. Those who desperately need Jesus need you to tell them the good news of God's love and grace. Hang in there! Don't give up.

Enjoy the rest of this book. Begin a dialogue with other volunteers and the leaders in your ministry. Ask good questions. Share your thoughts and insights. You and many others will be glad you did.

Survey Results

(Note: Each chapter concludes with specific responses to questions related to the chapter's subject matter along with appropriate statistics from a survey of more than 100 volunteers [see Appendix 1]. These are real responses from real volunteers.)

Volunteers shared the following one word responses to question #1 in the survey (see Appendix 1), "When I hear the word 'volunteer' the first word I think of is":

- "Service" or "servant" (number one response)
- "Helping" (second highest response)
- Other multiple responses included: "joy," "giving," "time," "work," "free" (no pay).
- A few single responses included: "compassion," "willingness," "wonderful," "older people," commitment," "opportunity."

Insight: Without question there is a right spirit among the surveyed volunteers saying, "I am *serving* as a volunteer to *help* others." These volunteers are committed to people. Not once were the words "program," "project," or "task" suggested. The good news is that ministry volunteers in our current culture seem to be *getting it right*.

In response to the second part of question #1, there were multiple positive responses from volunteers, sharing their best memory of being a volunteer. One of my favorites was, "I shoveled mulch for two days on a farm in which the owner had a bad injury."

Question: If you could add another word to the above question, what would it be?   .

Chapter 1

Developing a Relationship with Your Leader

Elijah was a man just like us.
(James 5:17)

Paid leaders are human beings. They have the same
desires, dreams, and demands as most volunteers.
They are not superhuman. Each night they put their head
on the pillow just like you and me.
(Doug Fagerstrom)

Remember your leaders, who spoke the word of God to you.
Consider the outcome of their way of life and imitate their faith.
(Hebrews 13:7)

Servant leaders, on the other hand,
seek to respect the wishes of those who have entrusted them
with a season of influence and responsibility.
(Day 172, Online Devotional from Lead Like Jesus*)*

Introduction

Bob got it right from day one. As a volunteer, Bob determined he was going to have a relationship with Jim, the youth leader in his church. Bob took the first step. He asked to have coffee with Jim. While they met at the local watering hole, Bob asked question after question about Jim's call to ministry, his personal life, and his goals for the youth ministry. Every question led to more questions, more stories, and more points of connection that required another lunch and later, dinner with spouses.

During those initial conversations more than ministry occurred. A relationship was born. It was personal. It was healthy. Bob learned to love and respect Jim, and Jim learned to love and respect Bob.

Before long, Bob's phone began to ring. When Jim called, the request was not always related to church ministry, but for personal help taking down a tree in his backyard or a canoe trip into a popular fishing spot within their state. After a while, there was nothing that Bob and Jim would not do for each other.

What these two men developed was more than memories. They fostered respect, honor, and appreciation for each other. They shared God's Word out of their personal devotional lives. They learned to challenge each other to be godly husbands and fathers. The needs of the ministry became second nature, and the two served the young people in the church as a model team, recruiting, impacting, and including other volunteers.

Your Leader and You

Many people don't remember their leaders because they had no relationship. For some volunteers, the ministry leader was only a role, a title, or a distant person out in front who had a relationship with others, but not with them. Without a relationship between volunteer and leader, there is little activity. With little activity there are few to no memories. Therefore, relationship is necessary to ensure activity as well as memories.

This first chapter is crucial for the volunteer. It is one of those "make or break" realities. If you never have a relationship (working or personal) with your leader, your volunteer role will most likely disappear as you distance yourself from the ministry and move in another direction. Only time will prove that to be a reality. On the other hand, an open relationship with your direct leader or supervisor will foster healthy communication and meaningful outcomes at the end of every ministry encounter. If the leader is pursued so will be the role you are assigned. If the leader is avoided, so will be the ministry in your heart and mind. It will also be avoided on your calendar.

Ten Imperatives for a Leader and a Volunteer

1. Always tell the truth.
2. Be careful how you talk about others.
3. Learn to ask lots of questions.
4. Learn to listen to each other.
5. Practice the fruit of God's spirit. (See Galatians 5).
6. Have fun with each other.
7. Share prayer requests.
8. Pray about the ministry together.
9. Don't wait for the other to take the first step.
10. Encourage each other by saying, "Well done!" or "Good Job!" or "I Appreciate You!"

Identify Your Leader

So, the first step is to clearly identify who you report to. While this sounds so basic and almost insulting to you right now, it does not for some. Some organizations do not make it clear where the volunteer reports and finds direction. It is confusing when you are to report to multiple personnel. It is frustrating when it is unclear to whom you are to report. Ask the question, "To whom do I need to go for clear directions and resources to fulfill the role or task ahead of me?" That should point you to the right person. Keep asking for leader clarity until there is but one person that you are confident will be guiding you through the ministry.

Respect Your Leader

"Respect" is one of the most important words in any relationship. In some cases it may precede other relationship words like "love," "honor," and "care." In the New Testament "respect" has three meanings. One of the Greek words, *phobos,* implies a virtuous responsibility of honor toward someone in a position of leadership (see Romans 13:7; Ephesians 6:5-7; and 1 Peter 2:17-18). Some texts will translate this word as "fear," as in "fear the Lord." However, showing proper respect (fear) for another person is not to run away in awful dread, looking for safety, but to run toward a leader with a sense of awe, admira-

> **Respect Means:**
>
> - Treating others with dignity.
> - Embracing differences and diversity.
> - Avoiding unkind comments or slander.
> - Building friendship and relationship out of love and genuine care.
> - Doing all of the above whether or not they are deserved.

tion, and honor. It is within that kind of relationship that people can learn to feel safe and where trust abounds.

Respecting others includes serving alongside another with high esteem, honor, and a sense of reverence. It is all about finding in others values and virtues to admire and enjoy. At the end of the day, it means treating people with a sense of moral decency. Kindness and goodness are displayed in the person who has respect for others.

When a relationship of mutual respect develops, ministry becomes delightful. Personal and community values are enhanced. Warm connections follow. Lives are transformed within the ministry, and those outside the ministry will notice that. Here are a few suggestions to build a relationship of respect with your leader:

- Get to know your leader by asking questions about his or her personal life and commitment to the ministry. Honor your leader by believing he or she is the leader for many reasons and that others have recognized those good reasons. In other words, discover why your leader is the leader.

- Offer to personally assist your leader with a task in which you can work alongside each other, rather than at a distance. You will learn much about your leader by working close together.

- Pause to reflect on and consider what your leader is facing in the way of personal or community responsibility. Try to put yourself in his or her shoes. Ask yourself, "What would I do if I were the leader?" Ask your leader, "How can I pray for you?"

- Complete simple assignments and tasks on time with a positive spirit.

- Don't engage in negative or damaging conversations with those who will complain about the leader (and everything else).

- Go out of your way to look for the things about your leader that are of good report and share those good reports with others (read Philippians 4:8, 9).

The Need for Trust

Trust happens mostly when there is face-to-face, two-way communication … and caring.

David Cottrell, Listen Up, Leader, *Page 17*

If Your Leader Is Difficult

At times, we will encounter and experience leaders who are not worthy of respect. Some leaders are not easy to work with or have difficulty getting along with people. Their idea of leadership is just to get the job done, and volunteers are simply a means to that end. Of course, that takes the joy out of volunteering. As one person said, "Difficult leaders are love-busters."

I have often shared this idea with paid staff, "When you can no longer respect your leader, it may be time to move on." For some, that is a very difficult statement to live out, especially if the leader has not earned the respect of the volunteers. However, if you are serving under a very difficult person and everything you attempt to do to establish a healthy relationship of respect becomes futile, here are several options to consider:

- Work through the situation. Patiently work through the difficult times with a clear focus on what this ministry accomplishes. Pray about your heart and attitude toward your leader. Refrain from negative conversations with others.

- Talk to your leader. Gently confront your leader about some of the difficulties you are experiencing. It may be that the leader has certain blind spots and will appreciate that you pointed out these difficulties to him or her. If your leader does not respond well to your honest and constructive comments, it may be a good sign to move to another area of service.

- Make a ministry change. Move on to another ministry, working with another leader or team. If you are chafed every time you enter the ministry context with a leader you cannot respect, you will not be effective, and the other members of the team will be negatively impacted.

- Examine yourself. Consider your own heart and attitude. Ask God if you are the source of difficulty. If your personality or spirit is in conflict with a leader, it may be that you are the one who needs to adjust your thoughts and objectives. Maybe your expectations of your leader are unrealistic. If so, bring those ideals into an honest attitude of respect and admiration for the leader. Ask God to help you work together.

The above list is not all-inclusive, but it may provide some good starting points for you to begin regaining respect for a difficult leader. It is God's desire that you serve wholeheartedly. Seek that with all your heart.

You and Your Leader

Presenting Yourself to Your Leader

Tell your leader what he or she can expect of you. I have learned to share with those I work with, "I am not a good mind reader." It is difficult to know what other people are thinking, especially in a working environment. The key to solving this dilemma is good communication.

Some leaders find it difficult to ask volunteers to meet certain expectations. They feel tentative about requiring too much of a volunteer, or they live in fear of losing the volunteer. (Of course, there are other leaders who are not shy at all about demands and requirements of you as a volunteer.) Letting a leader know what he or she can expect of you can reduce this potential tension. Don't expect a kind and tender leader to be able to guess what you are willing to do in the ministry. Make your intentions and boundaries simple and clear. Here are ten things that a leader would love to know about your role and level of commitment:

1. I will commit to serve ___ hours per week.

2. I will serve from _____ (month) through _____ (month).

3. I will commit to this ministry role for _____ (period of time).

4. My first priority(ies) that may preempt my service responsibility is (are) _____.

5. I am/am not willing to attend extra meetings that you may require.

6. I can/cannot give personal financial resources toward this ministry.

7. I will help you recruit people to serve with us and will participate in all training experiences.

8. I will be loyal to this ministry by speaking well of you and others.

9. If I experience any difficulties in serving, I will let you know right away. (Be willing to risk speaking "truth to power.")

10. I will give you plenty of notice if I decide to leave my role of service in this ministry.

Four Simple Ways to Earn Trust in a Working Relationship

1. **Keep your promises**. This can be the easiest of all trust builders but is often the most violated. If you say you are going to do something, do it. If you commit to being on time, be on time.

2. **Speak up.** Don't hold back what you believe would be helpful. You need to believe that you have the ability to see what a leader does not see. Be open and honest.

3. **Be consistent.** Erratic behavior can be problematic in a working environment. Leaders do not enjoy wondering every time if a volunteer is going to come through. Be dependable.

4. **Go above and beyond.** It is great to do what you say you are going to do. It is better to go one step beyond. It tells the leader, "I am really committed!"

Inviting Your Leader into Your World

Just as most volunteers love to be included in the life and plans of a leader, so many leaders enjoy being invited into the lives of their volunteers. It is much simpler for the leader to invite and include the volunteer(s) in his or her life and ministry plans. However, it is not always natural for a volunteer to include a leader into her or his life.

Let me encourage you to invite your leader into your world. Here are a few suggestions:

- Share your life story over coffee, lunch, or dinner. (You make the invitation.)
- Include your leader in a group event or gathering with other volunteers.
- Invite the leader to participate in your hobby, athletic, or family event (e.g., a promotional dinner at your workplace).
- Share your personal prayer requests in person or in a hand-written note.
- Inform your leader of your family's personal achievements or accomplishments (e.g., when your daughter or son is to receive an award at school).

I believe you will be pleased with the responses and results from your leader. While many leaders are busy and cannot respond to every volunteer's kind overtures, the invitation to your leader will go a long way toward building a healthy relationship that leads to mutual respect.

Asking Your Leader for Feedback

Do you want to grow? Do you desire to offer better service to others and to God? If so, healthy feedback is one way to engage the growth process. Sometimes, your leader may have great ideas for your ministry development and personal growth.

Some leaders will be hesitant to offer constructive feedback to volunteers. It is much easier to let a paid employee know what to correct, change, or do differently. It is not as easy to point out a weakness to a volunteer. The fear of losing volunteers keeps many leaders from being totally honest with volunteers who could improve their service in the ministry.

Six Questions to Ask Your Leader to Help You Grow

1. Am I meeting your expectations and the ministry's goals?
2. How could I do my role better or where could I improve my role and service?
3. Do you have any books or articles that I could read to do a better job?
4. Do you believe I am in the right role in this ministry or is there a place that you believe I could be more effective?
5. Have I done anything to offend or disappoint you?
6. Is there anything in my personal interaction with people in which I could improve?

Ask, "How can I grow?" Ask your leader what you can do to improve your work. First of all, the leader will be amazed at your level of personal maturity and security to ask that question. (The leader may respond with a bit of an inquisitive response, never having heard a volunteer ask such a wise question.) After the leader catches her breath, let her know that you are serious about honest, helpful feedback. (See sidebar with "Six Questions…to Help You Grow"). Set a time to do a simple evaluation. Do it in a casual environment when there is time for constructive dialogue with meaningful questions and responses.

Wanting Your Leader to Be Himself

"Leader, I need you to be you so I can be me."

How a leader acts is often how those who follow will respond and act. A leader sets the pace and tone for the ministry environment. Encourage your leader to be open, honest, vulnerable, and real. If he or she is, you will tend to be the same. A productive ministry environment oozes open, honest communication. Ask your leader to create a transparent place of ministry.

Sometimes leaders feel they need to create a particular image that is perfect and precise. Give your leader permission to be wrong. Let your leader make mistakes. Let your leader be the human being that he or she is.

Help your leader be real and genuine. Here are a few ideas to help your leader relax and not feel the pressure to be artificial and surreal.

- Encourage your leader when a mistake is made; don't criticize the error.
- Give encouragement to your leader when a step of courage is needed.
- Remind your leader that you are not going to bail out if circumstances are difficult.
- Ask what brings your leader the greatest joy and greatest concern.
- Talk with your leader about everything—the good, the bad, and the ugly.
- Let your leader know when you make a mistake. Own it. Take responsibility. (If you appear perfect, some leaders think they need to do the same.)

Praying for Your Leader

It is often said that one of the most intimate times that two people can share is when they pray together, aloud. When two or more people come together into the presence of an almighty God in His throne room of grace, it becomes a holy and spiritual moment. It is there that God promises grace, mercy, and help in our time of need (Hebrews 4:16).

Three Prayer Requests to Ask Your Leader

1. How can I pray for your role and the demands on you in this ministry?
2. How can I pray for you and your family and others in your life at this time?
3. Are there items of praise and thanksgiving for which we can give credit and glory to God?

Note: These requests may come singly or all at once. You may ask your leader face to face for prayer items. Or, send your leader the above requests through an e-mail or personal handwritten note.

Every leader needs grace, mercy, and help. Be confident that your human leader has needs that require divine assistance. Remember that your ministry supervisor does not just wrestle with flesh and blood but with the unseen forces of evil in this fallen and broken world (Ephesians 6:12).

Your leader needs your prayer support!

Because prayer is rather intimate, it may not always be simple or easy to pray with a leader. However, it is a wonderful goal to move toward. It may be best to invite another volunteer to join you in asking to pray with your leader. There is some comfort with more than just you and the leader. Here is a suggestion for approaching your leader:

> *Jane, Susan and I were wondering if we could take just a couple of minutes to pray with you. We have a number of things that we would like to thank God for, and we would like to commit this new area of ministry to God. Would it be okay if Susan and I prayed right now?*

I have to believe that your leader will be encouraged and enriched like never before. The other day, I received the most encouraging e-mail from a friend. The e-mail simply read, "I prayed for you today." That made my day!

Survey Results

In question #13 in the survey volunteers were asked to describe the relationship they have with their leader. Here are a number of their responses:

- "Good," "great," "friendly," and "close" were among the four most positive responses.
- "Fair," "OK," "open," and "limited" formed a second category of rather neutral responses.
- "Strained," "distant," and "confusing" marked a few negative responses from volunteers about their relationship with their leaders.

In the same question (#13) the volunteers were asked to describe the relationship they would *like to have* with their leaders. If the relationship was positive, the response was mostly the same. If the actual relationship was negative, the desired relationship was positive (e.g., if the actual relationship was "good," the volunteer described "good" as what would be desired in the future. If the actual relationship was "distant," the desired relationship was "close.") No volunteer desired a negative "distant" or "strained" relationship to continue.

Insight: Healthy, mature relationships are important to volunteers. It may be the responsibility of some volunteers to initiate dialogue with a leader to improve a less-than-best relationship. Of course, the risks of approaching a leader need to be considered. On the other hand, the benefits need to be considered equally also to encourage a healthy, honest conversation.

Question: If you sense or feel that a distance exists between you and your leader, would you be willing to ask him or her what you can do to create a closer ministry relationship?

In question #20 in the survey, volunteers added information about the relationship with their leader:

- 39% indicated they would like to spend more time with their leader.
- 49% indicated an uncertain "maybe" to spending more time with their leader.
- 12% indicated no interest in spending more time with their leader.

In the other half of question #20, 54 percent indicated they would like the leader to be involved in their lives, while the others said they were not really interested. However, no one said "no" to allowing the leader to be more involved in his or her life.

Insight: Volunteers are open to spending more time with their leaders. However, it does not seem that more time is the issue. Honesty, trust, and a quality relationship of respect seem to be higher values than a "best friend" scenario.

In question #4 in the survey, volunteers were asked to indicate the frequency that a leader prays *with* them. Here are the results:

- 28% indicated "often."
- 35% indicated "occasionally."
- 27% indicated "seldom."
- 7% indicated "never."
- 3% did not respond to the question.

In the second part of question #4, volunteers were asked to give their open response about what happens when leaders pray with them. All of the responses were positive: "joyful," "blessed," "encouraged," "grateful," "fulfilled," "energized," "contented," "comforted," "appreciated," "inspired," "humbled," and more. However, those who indicated that a leader had not prayed with them did not respond favorably.

Insight: There is no question that volunteers respond well to a leader's time of prayer with them. In other words, more prayer between leaders and participants is very positive. It is good and healthy for the ministry when leaders and volunteers pray together.

Question: Can you and a couple of other volunteers initiate together a prayer time with your leader? The survey indicates you will be glad you did.

Chapter 2

Becoming a Ministry Partner with the Rest of the Team

I commend to you our sister Phoebe, a servant of the church in Cenchrea. I ask you to receive her in the Lord in a way worthy of the saints and to give her any help she may need from you, for she has been a great help to many people, including me.

Greet Priscilla and Aquila, my fellow workers in Christ Jesus. They risked their lives for me. Not only I but all the churches of the Gentiles are grateful to them.

Greet Mary, who worked very hard for you.

Greet Andronicus and Junias, my relatives who have been in prison with me. They are outstanding among the apostles, and they were in Christ before I was.

Greet Urbanus, our fellow worker in Christ, and my dear friend Stachys. Greet Tryphena and Tryphosa, those women who work hard in the Lord.

Greet my dear friend Persis, another woman who has worked very hard in the Lord.
(Romans 16:1-4, 6, 7, 9, 12)

"Team" is just today's term for what the Bible describes as giftedness exercised in community.
(Nancy Ortberg, Leadership, *Spring 2008)*

All through the ages of the Christian church Paul has received a lot of credit for his pioneering work in advancing the gospel of Jesus Christ and building up the church throughout the known world. I confess that when I read the above names and brief descriptions of Paul's ministry hall of fame, I am reminded that we are not alone as leaders in this great endeavor called ministry. Paul did not do the work of ministry alone. He had help. He had lots of help. Read the above list of women and men again.

As I recall my many ministry relationships, I rejoice in the hundreds of people who shared in my ministry life. I am reminded of a group of men with whom I shared a two-year ministry relationship. I was a full-time staff person in the church, and they were all volunteers. Together we studied the Bible. Together we prayed and shared our lives with one another. Together we remodeled a house in the inner city of our town for a needy family. Together we got dirty, sacrificed family time, and gave of our personal resources. I think each one of us left a few drops of blood (literally) somewhere on that housing project.

The good news is that what we did was never announced, and pictures were never shown in our church. No one really emerged as "the leader." We were co-laborers, equally carrying the load. God quietly received all the glory. There is no question that we were all volunteers. God led us to work on this house through another ministry. We had total permission to tear down walls, add

---

A Leader's Apology

Forgive me for not trusting and believing in you as a volunteer.

Forgive me for not believing that you could do the job better than I.

Forgive me for planning everything by myself and demanding that you meet my expectations.

Forgive me for taking advantage of your time and resources to serve my agenda.

Forgive me for the many times I ignored you, walking past you without asking how you were doing in your personal journey… I am ashamed.

Forgive me for saying only, "Thanks" and not saying, "Good job, well done, way to go!"

Will you please forgive me?

a kitchen and bathroom, repaint, re-carpet, resurface, re-side, and re-roof the entire house. It was hard work. We did it together and now we have the best memories.

We were partners. We all shared in the same work. Some had more carpentry expertise than others, so we assisted those with the better skills. Sometimes, I did nothing but hold a cupboard that was being installed by a more gifted volunteer. Everyone was a worker. Everyone was a leader.

As I look back, I see that no one took the credit. Even though I was the staff member, the project was not mine. Some of the young men were board members; others were not. Some served in other leadership capacities in the church. Others had no clearly defined role in the church. We were equal in heart, soul, and mind. We needed each other's strength. When our own muscles could not lift a wall into place, we relied on one another. That project was, and still is, a living reminder of how we should always serve God and one another, as a team, as partners. We served wholeheartedly, as a group.

As A Volunteer, You are Valuable To This Ministry

As a volunteer, you need to believe and understand that you have great ideas and can make a great contribution to the ministry. Believe and understand that your heart and life can be just as engaged and committed as that of the leadership. If you have been around for a number of years, understand that you have a perspective of the history, needs, people, and potential of this ministry that others may not have.

This ministry needs you. It needs your giftedness, insights, and perspectives. But, it needs more than your time, talent, and treasure. It needs everything God has given you. Bring it to the table. Serve others with all that you have. Remember: *wholehearted devotion!*

So, what specifically do you bring to this ministry? Here are a few thoughts. You bring:

- Personal commitment and a desire to serve here and not somewhere else.
- A unique background and a lifelong heritage that is different from anyone else's.

- Certain victories and failures that can become teaching tools for the community.
- A mix of God-given spiritual gifts and talents.
- A God-shaped spiritual journey to help shape your community of faith.
- A personality, viewpoints, ideas, convictions, and insights that are yours alone.
- Special interests and experiences that have been regularly shaped by your reading, relationships, and individual discoveries.
- Freedom and flexibility that paid employees often do not enjoy.
- Extra energy that comes from the stimulation of your career, family, and more.
- Love, joy, and peace along with the rest of the fruit of God's Spirit.

Now, look for ways you can give all of the above and more to the place where God has called you to serve. Sharing those things is the joy of the believer. Others will appreciate it.

You Are a Partner.

The large national chain department stores now call their employees "associates." I think they are attempting to raise the involvement and commitment of every paid person to contribute more. There is a new desire on the part of employers to foster a sense of employee ownership and involvement that goes beyond the hours served and the tasks performed. I believe that attitude is growing in many ministry contexts. Partnership is not a new word. But, it is being used more and more.

By simple definition, a partnership is a cooperative agreement between individuals who consent to carry on an enterprise while contributing personal resources, resulting in a common outcome, sharing in the success or failure of the final results.

A healthy partnership begins with a clear understanding of the desired future (clear vision toward stated goals and objectives). Healthy partnerships openly and sacrificially share personal resources without concern for personal return or gain. Though individual goals may be achieved in a partnership, the community's mission is more important than personal outcomes. A partnership can be two or more people. You will know when the team becomes too large and you lose the sense of partnership or mutual exchange.

> ## A Partner is
>
> a cooperative participant, serving toward an agreed outcome and giving mutually agreed upon resources to a common goal with equal responsibility for the results.

Partnership is all about coming together. It does not happen by itself. It does not thrive or grow in a vacuum. Partnership is not completing someone else's list of tasks. Successful partnerships are dynamic with a desire for all partners to think, contribute, and grow beyond where they are today, while accomplishing an objective that only *we* can accomplish.

Better Together

Do you believe that together is better? God seems to say that partnership is superior to other organizational motifs. Here are a few familiar examples:

"It is not good for man to be alone. I will make a helper suitable for him" (Genesis 2:18). From the early days of creation, God saw that we need to live and love in partnership, not as independents.

"Two are better than one" (Ecclesiastes 4:9; read vv. 8-12). God could not be clearer. The context is about a man who has neither a son nor brother to help him with his work. Two working together have a better return for their work. Two are better than one.

"As iron sharpens iron, so one man sharpens another" (Proverbs 27:17). We need direct input and insight from others to improve our impact on the world entrusted to us.

"He who looks after his master will be honored" (Proverbs 27:18). Here the servant of God works in close relationship with a leader. Neither can function independently. The leader needs the help of the servant. The servant does well to work closely with the leader.

In the New Testament, Jesus referred to the yoke that binds a mentor and protégé together. Paul often carefully chose a partner to share his missionary travels. *We* are in this together. Let's think and act that way.

We, Not Me

It seems that a new nomenclature is in order. If we are going to serve as partners, we can begin to talk about ministry with terms like "our" rather than "mine" and "we" rather than "I" and "me." While on the surface this thought may appear trite, it is meant to develop a very important heart attitude.

First, we are in partnership with God. That means God and I serve together with you. When I refer to "we" in ministry, it means, God, you, and me. When we place a sense of ownership in the work we share, it is no longer "mine" but it is now "ours"—God's, yours, and mine. That terminology can be very important in our conversations. It will live well in our prayers and discussions as we share ministry instead of just doing or claiming ministry as a personal agenda, event, or task to be performed. It is inclusive language, not individualistic.

Request a United Ministry Plan

Ministry, by nature of its mission and objectives, should be far more open and inclusive of people than other organizational models. Ministries can create open highways for everyone to participate and have input at every level of decision-making.

It is unfortunate when only a few people are involved in the proverbial "inner circle" of ministry. Sometimes a narrow governance structure develops because of certain ministry demands or the basic structure formed by the founding fathers. Other times, people tend not to get involved in the ministry plan because they never thought they could.

Today, many growing ministries value the input of their volunteers. They really want to hear from them but don't always know the best way to open the door. They need your help to do that.

A United Ministry Plan simply states very clearly where staff and volunteers fit into the overall development of the ministry and ministry outcomes. The Plan can begin with a few easy-to-answer questions. Share these questions with your leaders:

- Would you like our (volunteer) input? This is always the first question.
- What is the desired outcome of this ministry project/ program?
- Is there anything that leadership feels is lacking and would desire to see more of to meet our objectives?
- How can volunteers become more involved in the ministry's future plans and decisions?

As a volunteer, request opportunity to have feedback and input. Suggest non-threatening ways to share ideas and opinions, such as open forums, suggestion boxes, or input into a newsletter. If those opportunities are granted, be kind, gentle, and positive. Use those means to be constructive and helpful to the community, not demanding or being divisive with negative overtones.

Work Together to Bless Others

The writer of Hebrews suggests that when believers meet together, we do well to stimulate one another to love and good work (Hebrews 10:24-25). The leader cannot do that alone. Don't assume that he or she is able to consider every need and show appreciation for every action. The leader is only one person and cannot do it all. Leaders need volunteers to learn to take care of one another. It requires a

---

United Ministry Plans Include:

- Open forums for all members to ask questions and share ideas.
- Quality comprehensive communication tools.
- Suggestion boxes and methods to survey and ask volunteers for input.
- Leaders who ask questions rather than just give directions.
- A community marked by patience and process that takes time to involve as many members as possible.
- Open celebrations when everyone gives thanks to God and honors one another.

team effort.

Psalm 1 is a powerful picture of how we can bless others. As a tree grows by a stream of water, it gives shade, bears fruit, and provides a setting of beauty and refreshment for everyone who passes under its leaves. Again, providing refreshment is something we can do together. Even the tree does not grow alone. Paul reminded believers in Corinth that some people plant seeds, some water the soil, and God brings the miraculous growth in people's lives. We are partners in blessing others.

Some members of a team are best at providing refreshment to other partners. They are natural encouragers and know how to lift up those who are down and provide strength to weary travelers. Some partners on a ministry team may not be the most gifted in accomplishing the task, but they are the best cheerleaders. I think of an individual in our church choir. He is not the most gifted singer. He will most likely never sing a solo (I think he should), but he encourages everyone who comes and is a prayer warrior for every need. He is a blessing!

Other partners in ministry know exactly how to bring the best out of fellow fruit bearers. They are always looking for the good in others and reminding ministry partners how important and valuable their gifts and presence are to the ministry team. They are the ones who are willing to step aside to give others an opportunity to serve. They are not thinking about themselves, only about the team and how each person can and should be given opportunities to grow.

Five Ways to Bless Other Ministry Partners

1. Send a kind note of appreciation to other volunteers.
2. Plan little celebrations for birthdays and other special days.
3. Offer to do someone else's job when you sense he or she is weary or overwhelmed with the ministry or with life.
4. Invite others into your life whether it is a dinner or special event.
5. Ask other volunteers how you can pray for them or their families.

What a blessing those partners become to the entire team.

The Volunteer's Role in Building Partnership Relationships

It is not up to the paid leader alone to build ministry team relationships. Each person will benefit from making meaningful contributions to bring everyone together. First of all, everyone is different. I know that is profound. But for some, when we start working together, we expect others to feel, think, and behave just like us. That is not partnership. And partnership takes work, hard work.

Partnership recognizes the contribution of the other partners and values their personal responses (feelings) and deep insights (thoughts). If you recognize the important value that you and each volunteer bring to the ministry, and share that with the leadership, soon they will begin to realize the valuable resource of knowledge and wisdom for the ministry present in the team.

Here are a several ideas for you as a volunteer to build up other volunteers:

- *Build relationships.* Get to know each other. Start with one other volunteer. Develop a relationship of mutual respect and honor. Ask questions. Share your backgrounds. Let each other know how committed you are to the goals of this ministry. Then add others to the discussion. Be a relationship starter.

- *Do your job.* Everyone has a role in the ministry, whether paid or volunteer. Once you have a clear understanding of what your contribution needs to be, do it (see chapter 5). Don't try to do the job of other volunteers, even if you think you can do it better. It is not your role. It is theirs. You may offer help, but only offer. Don't demean others by trying to do their jobs or telling them how to do them. Jim Collins in *Good to Great* suggests the importance of sitting in the right seat on the bus. Find your seat (role and responsibility) and celebrate that others have a seat on the same bus.

- *Honor others.* Learn to develop a high view of people. In hu-

Volunteers Are All Different

- Demanding Don: Everything needs to be his way.
- Relational Ruth loves everyone and couldn't care less about the details.
- Counting Curt is concerned about every little detail.
- Idea Inez has a new idea at every gathering. She loves change.
- Historic Herb: Don't mess with what has always worked before.
- Hasty Harriet: Fast paced, impulsive, impatient, and always talking.
- Systematic Sam puts everything in order with a system, list, and timeline.
- Corporate Carol has a spreadsheet and marketing plan for every program.
- Lazy Luke: He is along just for the ride, free food, and good times.
- Spiritual Sandy is all about prayer and what God has to say.
- Financial Fred counts the cost.

mility consider others better than yourself (Philippians 2:3). Do not be consumed with what they think of you, good or bad. That is not your assignment. Your God-given task is to enhance the reputation of others. Be the one volunteer on your team who is known for telling everyone else he or she is doing a great job for Jesus and the kingdom of God.

- *Grow others.* Quietly come alongside other volunteers and share how you are growing in your spiritual life. Let them know how important it is to you to read the Bible, pray, and give yourself to others. Remember, some volunteers are baby believers. The idea of serving God may be brand new to them. They need you to help them grow.

- *Celebrate.* When you see God do something big or small, be the first to give Him the credit. Keep reminding the other partners on your team who is really in charge (God) and who really gets the credit (God) for what is happening in people's lives. Be known as a "celebrator" rather than a celebrity.

• *Ask questions.* Be the person who asks good questions in both good and difficult times. When a ministry struggles, many participants complain, hold back, or run for the hills. You can be a volunteer who patiently asks gentle questions along the journey. Some questions to consider might be:

o How can we pray for our leadership and the ministry needs?
o What can I do to help during this time of special need?
o Where do we go from here? How can we move forward?
o Have we been here before? Can we learn from the past?
o Can we all come up with one or two ideas to make a difference?

Be the volunteer that brings people together during tough times, rather than the one who might divide.

Recruit Others in the Ministry

Healthy partners recruit other partners. One of the biggest responsibilities in any ministry is recruiting more volunteers. If a ministry is seeking to meet its mission, it needs more people to serve. In addition there is the natural attrition of volunteers. People get sick; some burn out; others move away. They need to be replaced.

The best recruiters of volunteers in any ministry are volunteers. As a volunteer you know better than anyone else what it means to serve in this ministry. You can often answer a volunteer's questions better than a leader can. You are there. You do the work.

Offer to help your leader recruit future volunteers. First, request from your leader some brief written summaries or a brochure of the ministry role seeking workers. Second, present them to a friend or a referral for the ministry. The materials give you credibility as a recruiter. Invite the future volunteer to join you in your ministry role. Finally, share feedback of the visit(s) with your leader.

As a volunteer recruiter you are building the ministry. God can use you to multiply your work, dream bigger dreams, and envision what God may do in His kingdom. Isn't it exciting to see all the ways you can partner in this great endeavor called ministry?

Survey Results

In question #6 in the survey (see Appendix 1):
 75% indicated they prefer serving on a team.
 25% indicated they prefer serving alone.

In question #14 in the survey, 35% indicated they found courage to serve when working in a team situation.

Insights: Overwhelmingly, the majority of volunteers prefer to serve in a team-nurtured environment. But there also are a few "lone rangers" in ministry who do not always do well in a team. It is important to recognize that not everyone fits into a team.

Question: What type of volunteer roles in your organization work best for those who cannot work well on a team?

Chapter 3

Knowing the Ministry

Please talk to me… don't ignore me.
When I talk to you, please show that you are listening…
even a little. If I initiate communication,
would you kindly entertain my request?
(A Committed Volunteer)

I myself am convinced, my brothers, that you yourselves
are full of goodness, complete in knowledge and competent
to instruct one another. I have written you quite boldly on
some points, as if to remind you of them again, because
of the grace God gave me to be a minister of Christ Jesus
to the Gentiles with the priestly duty of proclaiming the
gospel of God, so that the Gentiles might become an
offering acceptable to God, sanctified by the Holy Spirit.
It has always been my ambition to preach the gospel where
Christ was not known, so that I would not be building on
someone else's foundation.
(Romans 15:14-16, 20)

The Apostle Paul was committed to clearly communicating his ministry to those who were his partners in ministry. He shared his beliefs, passion, convictions, and motives. Followers in Rome knew Paul's mission and future plans. There was no guessing what the leader had in mind for the ministry. In the first verse above, Paul demonstrates the importance of clear communication and believes that the "volunteers" in the church at Rome are capable of instructing each other and are competent to partner with him in the gospel. He knows he does not have to be present for the church to survive.

Several years ago, I was asked to coach a pastor and his struggling church in developing a vision and plan for the future. We discovered very early that the leadership did not communicate well with the members. While the staff and board knew everything that was going on, unhappy and frustrated volunteers were leaving the church faster than new volunteers could be recruited and trained.

The chairman of the board did a very gutsy thing. He decided to start posting the minutes of the board meetings in the foyer of the church. That had never been done. The board members and staff were rather leery of the bold action, but it was the right thing to do. Within a few short months, people were engaged in conversations about the future of the church. They felt respect and trust from the board and staff, and they, therefore, developed respect in return.

This was the church where many of the dedicated volunteers had grown up. This was the ministry in which they sacrificed their time and resources and to which they pledged a personal commitment during difficult days. The people did not want to be on the outside looking in, nor did they want to meddle or control the leadership. They just wanted to be integrated into the process and be aware of the information that was being discussed by leadership.

Volunteers simply want to know what is going on in their ministry. They want to be partners. Most often their desire is to serve wholeheartedly, but that is difficult when they have only partial information and lack understanding of where the ministry is and where it is going.

Communicate. God Does. So Should We.

God calls it revelation. He has revealed Himself to us through creation, the Bible, and the person of His Son, Jesus Christ. We see the evidence of God's revelation in the lives of His children, believers in Christ, and through many miracles and answers to prayer every day. God is always communicating to us. He is never silent. Just look outside a window. God is saying loud and clear, "I am here and I love you!"

Volunteers will do well to share the same message. It is good to say, "We are here and we love you." Volunteers need not hide quietly in the cloistered corners of the ministry. God has given us tongues to speak and ears to listen. Leaders need to hear what you are seeing, thinking, perceiving, and understanding. Leaders cannot read minds. Sometimes they get too busy to stop and listen. But, don't let that keep you from considering ways to share your thoughts, ideas, and concerns. Here are a couple of ways that volunteers can communicate:

- Talk to leadership face-to-face. Most will be delighted that you are willing to ask questions and carry on a dialogue that addresses their concerns and yours. It may surprise you to know how much you are on the same page.

- Talk with each other. Learn what is going on in each other's lives and ministries. Share the good things that God is doing. Make discoveries by asking questions. Don't be silent.

Learn to be upfront and personal rather than distant and invisible. I have never heard a leader say, "The volunteers in our ministry talk too much. They have comments about everything." However, I have heard leaders say, "I wish we knew what people are thinking. We know they have thoughts, opinions,

Have You Heard...

- The names of this ministry's legends?
- Hilarious stories of the past?
- Tribal rituals or taboos?
- Embarrassing stories of the past?
- Stories of young people who were impacted by this ministry and went on to do great things for God and others?

and ideas. We just don't know what they are."

It would be easy to read the leaders' comments and say, "They should ask us what we think. They should not walk around, wondering what is on our minds." While that is a great observation, we need to be reminded that some leaders just don't know how and when to ask those important questions. Many leaders are very busy, and their minds are consumed with other personal thoughts and ministry needs. I will admit that some leaders just don't ask volunteers what they think. But, that should not preclude volunteers from sharing the first question or thought about their perceptions and insights on the ministry.

Talk About the Past

Learn the history of your ministry. Discovering the roots, foundations, and formations of the founding visionaries can help bring clarity and understanding to many of the "why" questions. Why do we function the way we do? Why do we meet when and where we do? Why does this facility carry this name? Why do we limit ourselves to this or that? Why do we believe what we teach? Many times a church or para-church ministry began with a very specific mission. Understanding that mission can be of great value to embrace today's current objectives.

Do You Know...

- When the ministry was founded?
- Who the founders were?
- What was the original purpose and "mission field" at the beginning of the ministry?
- Are there any charter members?
- Where are former members?
- What was happening in the world when this ministry started?

A few young couples were complaining about the Sunday morning service schedule of their church. The eleven o'clock hour was becoming a difficult time to meet for them and their children. Then someone in the group shared that the time had been established more than 100 years ago because that was the only time the farmers could get to church after the morning chores. Under those circumstances, the time for an 11 a.m. service made sense. But now, a new time ought to be considered for the early-rising community of bus riders and corporate commuters who would prefer an early morning service, conforming to their daily routine of going to work before sunrise. The conversation started moving toward other days and evenings of the week. It is a new time and age of watching the clock and calendar differently.

The history of any ministry will be helpful for understanding current conditions as well as future directions. Here are a few ideas to learn the backdrop of the ministry you are participating in:

- Ask permission to dig through the archives. You will find fascinating pictures and stories in old brochures, minutes of meetings, and notes from previous participants.

- Spend time with some of the charter members or some of the older volunteers in the ministry. Warning: you may find it difficult to break away from the one question, "Would you tell me about the history of this ministry?"

- Go on the Internet and discover what was happening in your community and the nation during the early days of the ministry. It is amazing how culture impacts the direction of some ministries, whether for good or bad.

- Compare the ministry's history with that of other ministries in the general geographic area.

Talk about the Present

The current health and well-being of your place of ministry is very important. Therefore, it is necessary to discover the needs of the ministry today. This may be the easiest engagement of your exploration. It may also be the most exhilarating and, at the same time, the most challenging. The questions now move from "why" in the historical quest to the present questions of "what" and "how," such as:

- What is our current status with regard to people, finances, and facilities?
- What are the current demographics and needs of our people?
- What are we currently doing best, and what are our weaknesses?
- How do we make decisions?
- How do we process information and make plans for the future?
- How are we doing in accomplishing our mission?

Sometimes we take for granted our present surroundings. We get into ruts and routines and mindlessly go through the motions. Old habits and unhealthy perennial patterns keep many communities from maturity and a focused mission. All of that gives reason to ask

---

Do You Know...

- The names and positions of the current ministry staff?
- The present budget and whether the ministry is financially ahead or behind?
- What is the greatest human resource need of the ministry?
- Who to contact…to share a prayer request?…to find a phone number?
- The name of the board chair? treasurer?

---

important questions. Healthy questions, asked with right motives, can bring positive results.

As a volunteer, you would be wise to take a temperature reading of where you are at this time. Here are a few ideas to help you assess today's strengths and weaknesses as well as current opportunities.

- Ask present leaders how you can pray for the ministry.

- Ask people in the community who do not participate in the ministry for their impressions, knowledge, and reflections. Simply ask, "What is your impression of _____ (name of the ministry or special program)?" "What do you know or hear about _____?"

- Ask your children or other young people how they perceive the current conditions. Ask them why they attend the ministry. Ask what they like or dislike about it.

- Sit down with "old timers" and ask what they believe is good and what they wish would be changed. You will not be short of responses. Besides, those who have invested their lives in any ministry enjoy talking about the journey.

- Make some quick reflections on what is happening in your community's education, business, and government. Ask, "How are we addressing the needs that surround our ministry?"

After the questions and answers, take time to reflect and respond. Take the initiative to write down a few concluding thoughts and sit down with your leader and a few other volunteers to have an open dialogue on your findings. While remaining positive and supportive, the conversation can be extremely valuable.

Do You Know...

- The fastest growing area of the community?
- Other ministries that share the same mission and target audience?
- How many languages are spoken in your county?
- How many single parents live within five miles of your ministry location and what their average income is?
- The struggling and most successful businesses in town?
- The volunteer opportunities in your local hospital or health clinic?

Talk about the Future

Ask, "Where do we go from here?" I assume that you don't get in your car without knowing your destination. I believe you know where you are headed for vacation when you leave the house for those two weeks of rest and relaxation. We all want to know where we are going. It is one of the ways that God wired our personalities.

Discussing the future can be the most progressive and positive area of exploration. However, talking about the future is best delayed until there is a rather complete assessment of the past and present conditions of the ministry. Use the discussion of the future to dream, build compassion for people's needs, and stimulate unity among other volunteers and leaders.

Here are several discussion questions you can ask others about the future:

- What is our biblical mandate, and are we accomplishing the basics?
- What is our potential? What do others believe we should do?
- What do other people say we should do to serve them and our community?

- What have other ministries not done that we are capable of doing?
- What "out there" would really be exciting?
- What are we not doing that we could do or wish we could do?
- What biblical core values are not being realized?
- How would you complete this sentence, "I would like to see…"?

Do You Know…

- The ministry's mission statement?
- The bylaws and policies of the board?
- The board's annual goals or objectives?
- The budget needs or projections?
- The current ministry debt?
- The core values and statement(s) of beliefs?
- The current slogan or vision statement from leadership?

Conversations on the past, present, and future do not need to be in formal settings. In fact, a less-than-formal, relaxed setting sometimes creates the best atmosphere for everyone to be open and honest. These conversations are necessary times of discovery that can bring insight and encouragement to others in the ministry. Be the first to start the conversations. Leave the formal agenda behind. Just talk. We need more of that in our ministry contexts.

Why Do People Leave?

Another important piece of information to know is why people leave the present ministry. This may not be a pleasant topic for conversation, but it is significant. Ministries, like people, have different foibles, idiosyncrasies, and blind spots. Sometimes they are evident. Other times they are excused or overlooked. Often they are not addressed.

Healthy ministries identify, address, and remedy the shortcomings and unhealthy habits that tend to drive people away. It is good to know what they are. That is the place to begin.

Do Others Know...

- Who the volunteers in the ministry are?
- Volunteers' birthdays and anniversaries?
- Stories of volunteers and leaders?
- Special needs and requests of people in the ministry?
- Available street addresses, phone numbers, and e-mail addresses of the ministry team? (How about a photo directory?)

As a volunteer you might begin by asking yourself, "What might (or almost did) cause me to leave this ministry and go somewhere else?" Be honest with your answer.

The second question to consider is "What happened that encouraged a close friend to leave the ministry and go to the other side of town?" Try to evaluate that person's reason(s). Was it because of past, present, or future concerns? Was it a reason of personality, general belief, or distrust of leadership? Was the reason for departure circumstantial where feelings were hurt and irreconcilable differences created distance and conflict?

After you have the answers to those questions, ask if the problems can be remedied and changes made. Does the leadership know those personal responses from those who have departed? I believe they want to know, but often they are the last to hear the *real reasons* that cause departures.

Finally, ask your leadership what you and others can do to prevent future departures. Work together as partners to resolve some of the blind spots and ministry weaknesses. Offer to be a part of the solution. Don't settle for your own sudden departure.

Increase Communication

I will never forget hearing the statement, "A lack of communication increases imagination." I have learned to add a second line, "Increase in communication enhances innovation." In consulting with many churches, I have found that their number one weakness was a lack of communication. I expect to hear of that malady whenever I begin coaching a pastor or start a church assessment process. Leadership somehow misses the mark. How can volunteers make a difference?

- *Request communication tools.* Ask leadership to prepare material for a weekly or monthly news piece. It can be a simple letter on ministry stationery, an e-mail posting, or a brief handout at weekly gatherings. Anything is better than nothing. Suggest materials that could be a part of such a publication, such as important information, ministry stories, facts and statistics, or devotional thoughts.

- *Offer to initiate a communication tool.* It can be as simple as typing one story a week to be delivered to everyone. Here are a few other ideas:
  o Create an e-mail database of all constituents.
  o Create a monthly one-page newsletter with a set of address labels and stamped envelopes or send it out through a ministry group e-mail.
  o Develop a good old-fashioned bulletin board. (People do look at them.)
  o Ask the ministry for a roll of stamps and 100 note cards and begin writing notes to people on behalf of the ministry or leadership.

- *Suggest a town hall or open forum meeting.* It is amazing how people love to attend, ask questions, and hear leadership share the present and future state of the ministry. There is something special that happens when the community comes together to talk about where we are and where we are going. It is so simple to put such a meeting together. Offer to help. Then just do it.

- *Personal communication.* Learn to write letters, send note cards, and make phone calls. E-mail and text messaging are modern forms of communication, but there is still something missing when they are used. Just by writing this paragraph, I cannot communicate to you my passion, personal convictions, or high levels of energy that come through my tone of voice or non-verbal signals. Nothing is better than face-to-face communication. Set a goal to meet with one person from the ministry every month. Encourage others to do the same. Then, watch the spirit soar in your ministry because people are learning to know, love, and appreciate one another.

Survey Results

To questions under #7 in the survey (see Appendix 1): "Can you quote the mission statement?" and "Do you know the future direction of the organization over the next three years?" volunteers responded:

Mission Statement
22% said, "Yes, I know the statement."
63% said they knew the statement only "in part."
12% had "no clue" about the statement
3% did not answer the question.

Three-Year Direction
55% knew the future direction.
30% had a vague idea of the future.
5% were not clear at all.
10% did not answer the question.

For question #14 in the survey, "Purpose" was the number one answer to "What gives you courage?" More than 60% of the volunteers gave that response.

Insight: Knowing the purpose of the ministry is important to volunteers, but that purpose may not be known or often discussed. It appears that our ministries are doing a better job of sharing the vision for the future than sharing the purpose of the ministry. The importance of the ministry purpose needs to be raised to a new level.

Question: What do you think are reasons for the greater value on vision than on purpose?

From the two questions in #18 in the survey: *Every volunteer* surveyed indicated that talk about the future is important! The survey response was 100%. In addition:

- 79% of the volunteers surveyed said that knowing the ministry's history is *valuable.*

- 21% of the volunteers said that knowing the ministry's history is *interesting.*

- None of the volunteers said that knowing the ministry's history and future are unnecessary.

Insight: It is important to ask questions, interview old-timers, and get to know about the history of the ministry. It is even more important to talk about the future and where this ministry is going. It is difficult to do one well without doing the other. Because you are part of the future history and the bigger story of what God is doing in your ministry organization, talk about it with others!

Chapter 4

Communicating Your Ministry

They just don't know what they don't know!
(Familiar Saying)

Some of the world's best-kept secrets
are in the church of Jesus Christ!
(Something we all know)

I want you to know how much I am struggling for you and for
those at Laodicea, and for all who have not met me personally.
(Colossians 2:1)

In this note to other "volunteers," Paul is communicating what
he is experiencing in ministry and in life in order to partner,
encourage, promote prayer, instill unity, and to show believers
in Jesus how to live their lives as imitators of Christ.

The seventy-two returned with joy and said,
"Lord, even the demons submit to us in your name."
(Luke 10:17)

What a great ministry report! (Read Luke 10:1-17.) These early
missionaries were on an incredible ministry adventure. They had
few to no resources and their training manual was very thin. Yet,
God did some great things. It was very important to everyone that
they all came back and report to Jesus and each other the stories of
ministry. Other volunteers need to hear your stories too!

The opportunity to visit many different churches throughout the year is one of the delights of my job. As my wife Donna and I zigzag across our nation from week to week, we meet many people from a variety of backgrounds. Each one has a story.

I will never forget one church we visited. After I taught the Bible lesson on a Sunday morning, Donna and I were invited to a luncheon where we met with about twenty people from the church. As we met one new friend after another, I became overwhelmed with all the amazing stories. We heard stories about life and death, wealth and poverty, rags to riches, and riches to rags. Stories about hurricanes and personal holocausts were overwhelming. Some stories had us in laughter and others had us in tears. Yet, at the end of each story were the love and commitment of a volunteer ministry couple, Dan and Deanna, who had touched their lives and made a difference.

One outgoing woman with a thick New Jersey accent leaned over to my wife and said, "Everyone in this room has an amazing story." Our response was, "Then let the stories begin." We wanted to hear more stories. We could have stayed the remainder of the day, listening to one incredible, life-changing experience after another.

I am willing to guess that the majority of the people in that large southern church have no idea about all that God is doing in that group. While their quiet sharing (not for public attention) is a powerful picture of humility, I was reminded how we are obligated to share with one another what God is doing in our lives and through the ministry in which He calls us to serve. When we fail to remind others that there is a God who is great and full of love for His people, we keep secret what should be celebrated.

As the people of God, we need to learn to share what God is doing and what He is about to do in other people's lives. As we share our personal journeys, we become engaged and involved in one another's lives through intimate expressions of ministry and prayer. Let's love each other just the way the Bible tells us to. (Read 1 John 4 and 5.)

Share Your Personal Story

Your personal story needs to be shared. People want to hear what God is doing in your life. People in ministry want to know *you* first. Learning about the ministry is second.

A Volunteer's Story

Helen is an amazing volunteer. This octogenarian has the drive, dreams, and determination of a 30-year-old and isn't even thinking about slowing down. So, what is it that drives this high-octane grandmother? The simple answer: the Bible.

With the gift of teaching, Helen has taught the Bible her entire life. She has taught every age group in almost every state in our nation. If I were to mention the names of some of Helen's students, you might recognize them as well-known personalities, authors, and speakers.

With all of that acclaim, Helen simply loves teaching the Bible to her grandchildren and the constantly growing Bible study in her church. Yet, behind the influential teacher is a woman who is a loving wife, mother, grandmother, and dear friend to so many people. Helen is kind, caring, wise, whimsical, gracious, and gentle. She shows Jesus in all she does.

Being a great volunteer is not just about talent, but character and godly living. Helen is all of that.

A friend of mine said, "When people believe in you, they will more easily believe in what you have to say." The power in that statement is a reminder of how important our integrity and authenticity is to the people watching us. One's personal life is foundational to a ministry role. When I learn about your commitment to your family, God, and other people, I will have a better understanding and appreciation for your commitment to the ministry we share. It is time to get the word out.

Perhaps you're not comfortable sharing personal areas of your life. That is okay. You are in good company. Many of us struggle when the spotlight is on us. But, don't think of sharing your life as having a spotlight on you. Turn the spotlight onto God. Share your life by letting people know what God is doing and how you are enjoying His work in your life. Share one-on-one. Don't worry about sharing in front of a group.

Here are a few things people want to know about you. This list is not a "must share" list. It simply suggests areas from your life that will encourage others who partner with you in ministry. When they hear your everyday story, they will be more inclined to join you in ministry. Most partnerships are born out of relationships. This is a great place to start.

- Share your family background.
- Share when you began your faith journey.
- Share some of your previous accomplishments in school, work, or community service.
- Share when, how, and why you are involved in this ministry.
- Share one or two spiritual victories where you experienced the love and grace of God.
- Share a favorite and meaningful passage in the Bible or reflect on a pastor's sermon.
- Share a weakness where you are finding new victory.

Humbly and honestly let people know where you are in your life journey. Share a little bit of yourself from time to time. No speeches or sermons are necessary. It is time to be you and remind everyone what God has done.

Share Your Ministry Story

What God is doing in your area of ministry goes beyond what is written in a brochure or ministry newsletter. Do other people know

---

A Volunteer's Story

Roy is a senior volunteer. He faithfully serves each week in his church's Sunday School, takes a blind man shopping every week, and leads music in a nearby nursing home for the confined residents.

In addition, each day Roy visits his wife with Alzheimer's disease at another nursing home. During his daily six-hour visit, he offers to help the residents and nursing staff with a variety of chores. He is their number one volunteer every day. It seems that everywhere Roy goes, he is volunteering, helping others with anything he can do.

Recently, a younger man who visits his wife had been watching Roy serve so many people with joy and encouragement. The young man said to Roy, "Someday, I hope to be like you." Now, that is a volunteer.

your ministry story? Are they aware of what is happening in the lives of people whom you serve and pray for most every day?

Why share your ministry story? If others are going to become involved or engaged in ministry, your story may be the reason they see that they can make a difference as well. Some people have a view of volunteering in ministry that is high and lofty. Your story can make ministry real and personal.

A second reason to share your ministry story is to encourage those who are already participating in ministry. Some volunteers are discouraged or feel a bit abandoned or alone. Hearing your story gives them hope and a powerful reminder that God is at work. From your story, they can find courage to go back into their ministry and continue their story.

There are at least three people groups with whom you need to share the ministry you are serving. They are your leader(s); people who are in the church or para-church ministry, but not in your specific area of ministry; and people outside of the ministry in your community or other similar ministries. Once you have targeted the people you want to communicate to, here are few ideas of what people want to hear.

- Specific stories of changed lives.
- God's answers to prayer.
- Current trends, goals, results, and outcomes.
- Overall spirit and excitement of the people serving with you or the current major challenges. If you are sharing challenges or struggles, be careful not to share people's names who are the difficult participants. Share your struggles as prayer requests or seek advice from others on how to be more effective in your ministry.

People want to know what is happening. You don't need to be a great philosopher or executive leader. Just tell the facts and give God the glory.

Share Needs

It is easy to be shy and not want to report the needs that may be evident in your area of ministry. In our culture we attempt to fix the

A Volunteer's Story

Dawn asked God to give her an idea of how she could show love to the people at her job. Then the answer came: She would give a Valentine's Day party for the custodial staff.

So she baked cookies, made invitations, bought party favors and decorated her office. Everyone came at 8:20 p.m., on his or her break time.

It was a short party—only 15 minutes. But its glow carried over for a long time. The cleanup crew was amazed that anyone would honor them in such a way. Dawn made an impact on the people she works with. She carries fond memories of that Valentine's Day and the love of God she was able to share with others.

Dawn's story reminds us that volunteer ministry to others can be meaningful while being simple and inexpensive.

problems and present everything as being perfect. That is not always realistic. We cannot fix everything and nothing is going to be perfect. We need to invite others to help. That may begin with sharing the needs of the people in your ministry.

Sharing needs is not a sign of weakness. It is a sign of partnership. It sends a signal that you need other people and they need you. Ministry needs can become a point of personal engagement with others. Some will see the opportunity to help. Others will suggest additional resources. Some will pray. At some point, there should be a sense that we are in this together.

Here are some ministry needs that can be shared to involve the responses of others.

- People's needs in your area of ministry.
- Space and time constraints.
- Transportation requirements.
- Reporting, publicity, and communication expectations.
- Financial limitations.
- Additional help and assistance.
- Inter-ministry opportunities to work together with other areas of the ministry.

- Priorities and growth opportunities to expand the ministry.
- Any conflicts, crises, or inconsistencies perceived within your area of ministry.

Share the above list (and more) with the people who can make a difference. Sharing with "anyone and everyone" is not necessarily profitable for the ministry. The people in leadership need to know your needs. Others need to pray. Again, some will offer to help meet the needs.

Share Dreams

I love to dream. One of my favorite verses in the Bible is Ephesians 3:20. I am reminded that God is able to do anything He chooses. And what God does always exceeds my expectations and dreams.

Dreams are not just for leaders. I am convinced that you can have a dream and a great idea for your area of ministry. Because you are serving in the "trenches" and on the frontline of ministry, you will see what others do not see and can begin to imagine what only God can do. With a heart to see lives change, a commitment to the ministry, and with godly motives, a dream for the future is a good thing, a very good thing.

What Not to Share

- Don't share someone else's personal story without their permission.
- Resist sharing complaints about the ministry with people who can't do anything about the complaint.
- Resist sharing strong opinions that do not enhance the reputation of the ministry.
- Refrain from talking about a leader's or another volunteer's demise or downfall in your ministry.
- Hold back from sarcastic and demeaning comments about the ministry.
- Watch out for inflammatory, negative, and pejorative words that create unhealthy impressions.

I believe God has wired us to dream. After we define our ministry, develop an ongoing commitment, and discern certain needs, it is time to step back, pray, think about the ministry opportunities that are before us, and dream. The progression toward dreams can look something like this: Identify a ministry > Identify your role > Get involved > See the needs > Dream about the future.

One small note: Dreams and fantasies are different. I believe dreams are connected to real people, real needs, with real solutions and opportunities in mind. Fantasy does not always connect well in a real ministry context. Fantasies are the "Field of Dreams" found in childhood hopes and desires, which often are not aimed at impacting the lives of people for today and tomorrow. Although there is a place for fantasy, be sure to discern the fine connections where people will understand and relate to you and where you would like to see this ministry develop in the future.

Learn to Say, "Good Job"

In my book, *The Ministry Staff Member*" (Zondervan, 2006) I made the following point very clear. Saying, "Thank you" is often not enough.

After serving long and hard, after navigating through tough waters in ministry, the word "thanks" just doesn't cut it.

Some ask the question after receiving a nominal thank you, "*Thanks for what? For showing up? For doing what no one else would do? I don't think you really know what I did as a volunteer today.*"

Those real comments from volunteers remind us to learn to say, "Good job!" "Well done!" "Way to Go!" or "Atta-boy! – Atta-girl!"

Try them; you will see huge smiles.

Suggest a Celebration

Sometimes we get so busy, we forget to celebrate. The God of the Bible loves celebrations. If you read about the Old Testament festivals and "Grand Opening of the Temple," you will discover some of the greatest parties in the world. God loves a celebration that honors the work He is doing in your ministry. We will always do well to set aside times to celebrate God's goodness and give Him the credit for ministry results.

Celebrations can be on a grand or small scale. If you are inclined to design and develop an "all ministry" celebration, ask your leadership team for permission and get to work. However, if you are like me, you are more likely to participate in a quiet, brief time of giving thanks, showing gratitude to others and giving God credit in a small, more personal venue. Here are a few suggestions for your next "Good Job" celebration.

- Buy a congratulations card for someone.
- Bake or buy a dessert treat after a long difficult task is finally accomplished.
- Spontaneously take a hard working fellow volunteer to lunch or celebrate at their favorite coffee shop.
- Purchase a fun memento at the "Dollar Store" and see how much mileage it gets.
- Give a token of appreciation to a well deserving volunteer with the stipulation that they forward the same to someone else. See how far it goes (maybe unknowingly back to you).
- Okay, now it is your turn to think of a celebration idea.

You don't need permission to celebrate the goodness of God. Nike people might say, "Just do it." I like that. So, just do it. Celebrate!

Share with People Outside of the Ministry

The words of a 1960s pop song rang through a generation of bad news stories, "*Sure could use a little good news today.*" People love good news. While news of a fire or disaster sells newspapers, it is not what we want to hear. Your ministry is full of good news because a good God is at work.

Not long ago, I shared with my next-door neighbor one of our ministry stories at the seminary. While they have no direct link or involvement with the ministry, they were captured with my international update. They were interested to the point of asking questions and finding delight in some humorous anecdotes.

The Genius of One Minute

In sharing our stories, the *One Minute Manager Series* by Ken Blanchard is brilliant in form and concept. This great communication motif works better than you think. When you consider sharing the ideas and ministry topics in this chapter think about:

- One minute short stories.
- One minute half page written articles.
- One minute single view of screen e-mails.
- One minute to sign and send a card.
- One minute phone call to share a word of encouragement and say, "Good job."
- One minute visit to express a word of appreciation or encouragement.

One minute can last a long time!

Your ministry is no different. Actually, you will be quite amazed at people's interest in the stories that you have to share out of your ministry involvement. Try one. Listen for the warm response. Keep the report short and energetic. Try a little humor. Let the world in which you live share in the stories of God's goodness.

Here are a few people with whom you might consider sharing some of your stories.

- Your children, siblings, and extended family.
- Your parents (regardless of your age) will listen intently to your stories.
- Close friends in other areas of ministry.
- Send a note to the local newspaper. Maybe they will do a story on your ministry.
- Friends in other churches.
- Business colleagues and associates (great luncheon conversation).

You can always start with, "Hey, I have a great story about some people in my life. Do you have about three minutes for me to share an amazing (or out-of-the-box) story?" Then watch how one good story will lead to another. Maybe you will end up sharing the marvelous story of God, how He created, loves, and gave Himself for us. You never know.

Survey Results

In question #19 in the survey (see Appendix 1), volunteers were asked to share how they feel when given an opportunity to share their ministry with other people. Here are the responses, indicating that they feel: "excited," "empowered," "encouraged," "valued," "good," "blessed," "inspired," "grateful," "content," "honored," "humbled," "part of a team," "passionate," "privileged," "that we have accomplished something for God."

When asked in the same question, "How do you feel when people complain about the ministry?" there was a nearly unanimous response of volunteers' expressing sadness and sorrow. A few expressed disappointment about those who complain but do not become a part of the solution/team.

Insights: Letting others know about your area of ministry normally brings a very positive response both to the listener and to you, the storyteller. It is all about giving God the glory for what He has done. It is also a joy to know that God is using you to accomplish His mission in His kingdom.

Question: Have you given God praise for all He has done in your life as a volunteer in ministry? Have you shared that joy recently with others?

Chapter 5

Your Ministry Description Outline

Dear Leader, did you hear that I am frustrated?
Then you heard right!
Do you know why I am frustrated?
(Pause)

I didn't think you understood the reason for my frustration.
So, let me tell you why I am about ready to walk out that door.
First of all, I like you and I love this ministry. I would do
anything for the people we are serving. It is nothing short of a
childhood dream and life calling that brought me to this place.
However, I don't know what you want me to do!
Your expectations are unclear.
I feel that you expect me to read your mind or just figure this
out by myself. That's unfair and unrealistic. When I don't
seem to do it the way you wanted, you let me know your
disappointment through your sighs, critical feedback, and lack
of appreciation. You seem to forget I am a volunteer.
I have volunteered to sign up for this mission under your
leadership. Now lead. Just tell me what you want, and I will let
you know if I can do it. It is really that simple.
(A Volunteer)

A number of years ago, I attended a mega-church leadership training
conference. During the Saturday morning break I ventured out on

my own tour of the facility. I was amazed by the function and expansive space dedicated for ministry, especially for children and youth. While I was almost lost, meandering through several hallways and commons areas, I saw a gentleman on his hands and knees scrubbing baseboards with a rag and cleaning fluid.

I learned his first name and discovered that he was a volunteer at the church. I asked him if cleaning baseboards was his area of specialty and if that was his job every week. His response was a kind, "No." Then he went on to explain the very simple process volunteers follow each week as they come to serve the church with their gifts of helps and service.

In the custodial-maintenance offices of the church, there is a list of tasks that volunteers are requested to accomplish. The long list of custodial needs not only identifies the work that needs to be done, but notes what supplies are needed and where to locate those supplies. Numbered by priority, the items also have a notation indicating if a certain skill or physical requirement was expected. (e.g., "Fear of heights may be a concern." Or, "Fumes from the cleaning fluid may cause some skin or sinus irritation.") On the poster-board-sized list is a place for each volunteer to initial his name and note the time when the task is completed.

The volunteer I spoke with was positive and energetic about his volunteer work. He was eager to get back to cleaning the baseboards. He knew what to do, where to do it, and what to use to be successful in his role. (By the way, I learned he was the president of his own company, where he does not clean baseboards. But, he clearly knew his spiritual gift in the body of Christ, and he was using it to the glory of God.)

What Does Jesus Expect?

Jesus made His intentions clear for His disciples. His expectations were never filled with wonder or head-splitting confusion. The first job outline was clear, clean, and simple, "Come, follow me," Jesus said, "and I will make you fishers of men" (Mark 1:17). That's it. There was no list of twenty things to do, at least not yet. If there was any confusion, it was in interpreting the exact meaning of Jesus' words. The disciples needed time for teaching and training to grasp

Jesus' idea of the kingdom. Obviously, they figured the mission out in due time. But, Jesus never left His expectation ambiguous and without certainty. Jesus never changed the simple instructions (read John 21).

Jesus did not stop after He said, "Come, follow me." That would have been too open ended, vague, and unclear. If that is all Jesus had said, the disciples would have had every right to ask, "To do what, when, where, how, and why?" I am sure that, as fishermen, they were intrigued and mesmerized by this unique job description, to be "A Fisher of Men."

As Jesus taught and modeled His kingdom work with the disciples, He finally gave them a specific challenge and assignment. He called twelve of them (Luke 9) and then 72 (Luke 10) to go out to do the work of the ministry. He gave very clear instructions. He told them:

> The harvest is plentiful, but the workers are few. Ask the Lord of the harvest, therefore, to send out workers into his harvest field. Go! I am sending you out like lambs among wolves. Do not take a purse or bag or sandals; and do not greet anyone on the road. When you enter a house, first say, "Peace to this house." If a man of peace is there, your peace will rest on him; if not, it will return to you. Stay in that house, eating and drinking whatever they give you, for the worker deserves his wages. Do not move around from house to house. When you enter a town and are welcomed, eat what is set before you. Heal the sick who are there and tell them, "The kingdom of God is near you." But when you enter a town and are not welcomed, go into its streets and say, "Even the dust of your town that sticks to our feet we wipe off against you. Yet be sure of this: The kingdom of God is near."…He who listens to you listens to me; he who rejects you rejects me; but he who rejects me rejects him who sent me (Luke 10:2-11, 16).

After these instructions, there was not much left to one's imagination. Jesus outlined what to bring, what to do, and what to say. There was not a lot of guesswork in the assignment. (Go through the above text again and underline the action verbs that Jesus gave to the 72 volunteers.)

However, there were personal choices they could make. It was up to them as a duo to decide what town to enter and what home to approach first. After they entered a town and home, they were given a great deal of freedom and opportunity in how to love, live, and share with the people. While Jesus gave them a few words to say, He did not give them the entire script. He knew they would simply follow the example He had shown them in all of their previous encounters with the Master. And they did.

"The seventy-two returned with joy and said, 'Lord, even the demons submit to us in your name'" (Luke 10:17). I love that verse. First of all, they all returned. That is absolutely amazing to me. Second, they went beyond the basic job description. Jesus hadn't told them to bring demons into submission. But they did. What was that all about? I believe the disciples had enough understanding from Jesus' clear directives in verses 2-11 that when they encountered additional situations (demons, for example), they knew exactly what to do. They did what they had seen Jesus do when they followed Him around Galilee.

At the end of Jesus' earthly ministry He said these familiar words to the members of his body, the church: "Go and make disciples of all nations, baptizing them in the name of the Father and of the Son and of the Holy Spirit, and teaching them to obey everything I have commanded you. And surely I am with you always, to the very end of the age" (Matthew 28:19, 20).

As a result of those brief instructions, the world has never been the same. From just those few brief action verbs and clear directives, volunteers have given their lives for the mission of Christ. From two short verses in the Bible, mission agencies have been created to penetrate the dark corners of the world, and young people have shared Jesus with their classmates because they understood what it means to be a "fisher of men." Now, it is our challenge to arrive at the same level of clarity and simplicity to do the work of the ministry.

A Volunteer's Ministry Description Outline

For years we have called it a "job description." The term "ministry outline" gives a bit more of a general and softer tone to the expectations of the work to be accomplished. The ministry outline does just that; it gives the volunteer just enough of the general *outlined* expectations of what is needed to fill in the blanks. A good outline is usually constructed to complete the rest of the text more easily.

In writing this book, I painstakingly read and researched each topic and then prepared a detailed outline. Only after that did I have the joy of writing each paragraph and sidebar. I wrote the text from the outline. It is the same for a volunteer. You take your ministry outline and fill in the rest of the "text" when you begin the work and encounter the many situations and opportunities that could never have been noted in a long list of detailed tasks. You can always go back to your "outline" (ministry description) to make sure you are on the right "text."

Ministry outlines answer three basic questions:

- Can I do this job? (Qualifications)
- Do I know what to do? (Responsibilities)
- Who will be serving with me? (Relationships)

If there is one word to summarize the ministry outline, it might be "expectations." When we assume a role or perform a task, we are faced with certain expectations. A well-crafted ministry outline can make expectations clear and exciting.

A Leader's Expectations of a Volunteer

Qualifications

There always are specific qualifications for a volunteer to achieve his or her role in ministry. Every job has qualifications, at least initially. Every profession has clearly outlined criteria to assure that the worker is able to perform the job. Policemen, flight attendants, truck drivers, and doctors all have specific information they must know, abilities they must possess, and a level of experience that are stipulated as criteria in the job outline. Consider a few volunteer qualifications.

Personal commitment

Are you a member of this organization? Or, have you been attending the organizations functions/meetings for a specified period of time?

The Volunteer's Passion

As a volunteer, find your passion in people. Identify the people you are serving. Love them. Care about them. Get close to them and understand their lives, needs, hurts, and joys. When you do, you will find a new passion for what you do as a volunteer as never before.

Spiritual Gifts

Pastor and author Leith Anderson says, "A spiritual gift is a job from God." Most ministry roles require or presume at least one spiritual gift to function at one's optimal strength with a sense of deep joy and fulfillment. If you have not discovered your spiritual gift, it would be a good idea to ask your leader to help you discover your "job from God." It is a powerful and meaningful place to begin your quest as a volunteer.

Skills

Whether the area of service is a custodial role, teaching a class, or working in a kitchen, many volunteer roles require some basic or advanced skill levels. You will most likely bring either that skill to the role with you, or you will need the aptitude, time, and desire to learn the required skill. Keep in mind, there are some volunteer positions that require nothing more than your presence as in the case of a chaperone. However, even that has an assumed skill set, maturity and wisdom. Resist thinking you are volunteering only as a "warm body."

The Volunteer's Gift from God

Fan into flame the gift of God, which is in you through the laying on of my hands. For God did not give us a spirit of timidity, but a spirit of power, of love and of self-discipline. So do not be ashamed to testify about our Lord, or ashamed of me his prisoner. But join with me in suffering for the gospel, by the power of God, who has saved us and called us to a holy life—not because of anything we have done but because of his own purpose and grace (2 Timothy 1:6-9).

Training

Some ministries have unique roles and responsibilities that require a very specific skill, ability, or body of information. It is very important to ask your leader if there is specific education or training provided to do the job and do it well.

Background

You bring experience to the ministry that no one else has. It comes from your background. Your family of origin, unique experiences (good and bad), education, life roles (parent, child, leader, employee, friend, etc.), travel adventures, and more bring a wealth of insights and understanding to the serving community.

Personality

God wired you to be different from me. That is a good thing. It is also important if we are going to fulfill God's design for the body of Christ. If we all thought, felt, and acted the same, I don't believe the ministry would survive. But, together we can make a difference. I need to know what you are thinking and feeling through the people issues that we will encounter together. I could miss something that you intuitively see and I only objectively forecasted. Our unique individual styles and responses to life and ministry are high values to the community. Be you. I need you. Believe it or not, you need me.

Passion

Throughout my 35-plus years of ministry, I have come to understand that passion in ministry is related directly to people. I become passionate about people. I am passionate for my wife, my daughter, and my son-in-law. I have strong feelings and emotions for them. I am passionate about the faculty, staff, and students where I serve in my life's calling. There is nothing I would not do for each person at the seminary. As a volunteer, find your passion in people. Identify the people you are serving. Love them. Care about them. Get close to them and understand their lives, needs, hurts, and joys. When you do, you will find a new passion for what you do as a volunteer as never before.

Responsibilities

Most leaders have very specific goals they would like to see you accomplish. Sometimes it is very clear to them and to you what those goals are. When that is true, everyone is pleased and delighted with the results. At other times, you may discover the leader's expectations only as you go. Your discovery may be too late to do anything about them. Instead of joy and satisfaction, the results are hurt feelings, guilt, discouragement, and strained relationships.

As a volunteer you should have your responsibilities clarified in two ways. The first is a *general overview* of what is expected of you. This may be one or two (at the most) short sentences that refer to final outcomes and desired accomplishments. For example, "You are

---

Sample Volunteer Ministry Description
"Youth Ministry Sponsor"

Qualifications:
- Be a member in good standing.
- Demonstrate maturity and relational skills with a love for teens.
- Be able to attend 3 out of 4 monthly events in the youth ministry.

Responsibilities (General Overview):
Attend youth events and help oversee the needs of our teenagers in attendance at those events.

Specifically:
- Ride the bus to the events.
- Attend the entire event.
- Spend time participating in the events, talking with teenagers and establishing a friendship or parent-type relationship.
- Be available to teens with special needs.

Relationships:
- Report any special needs or problems to the youth pastor.
- Help other sponsors with light program tasks.

---

expected to organize and coordinate the annual fund-raising banquet." Or, "You are responsible for the weekly ministry dinner set up in the gymnasium each Wednesday before 5 p.m."

Embedded within that overview and general statement, there may be several *specific responsibilities* that you are expected to accomplish. For example, if you are responsible for setup in the gymnasium each Wednesday, you may also be required (more specifically) to:

- Set up 20 tables with tablecloths and 160 chairs.
- Set up four serving tables.
- Set up a small platform with a microphone.
- Be sure that a piano is near the platform.
- Recruit any help that is needed.

Learn in advance what is expected of you in the way of responsibility. Don't leave any responsibilities to the guessing game. It is not a fun game to play.

Serving Others

Sometimes you will be asked to serve alone. The task may be a solo role, which is just you and you alone. You may have the freedom to come and go as you please, or you may have specific tasks that can be performed only at specific times.

Other times you will have the responsibility to serve on a team. Some of those fellow servants will be your peers, working right alongside you, doing the same thing at the same time, like singing in a choir or ensemble. It is important to know your community responsibilities to be a part of the team.

Finally, there are people over whom you may have direct responsibility. Not every volunteer desires that role of accountability for others. However, if you are asked to take that responsibility, be sure you know what authority you have to help the people who are serving with you.

When serving as a volunteer, here are three good questions to consider:

- *To* whom am I accountable? (To whom do I report and answer?)

- *With* whom do I serve?
- *For* whom am I responsible? (Whom do I recruit and train for this area of ministry?)

Creating the Ministry Description Outline

Not every leader is going to sit down and write volunteer ministry descriptions. It just isn't going to happen. For those who do, give them a vacation trip to the Bahamas. They are the exception rather than the rule. Now, it is important for me to say, don't beat up your leader because he or she has not written ministry descriptions for you and other volunteers. Don't give her a hard time because she has not performed the ideal. Make this your opportunity to serve and assist your leader with something that is important and will be helpful to you.

Ask Questions.

Begin the ministry outline process by initiating a brief meeting with your leader. Let him or her know that you desire to fulfill the job as best you can and to the glory of God. Encourage the leader that you need a little more information to understand the role fully in order to do the job completely.

Remind the leader that you want some of this information rather soon, so you won't have to keep coming back again and again to com-

---

Why Some Leaders Don't Write Ministry Descriptions for Volunteers

- It takes a lot of thought and time, and leaders of volunteers are some of the busiest people on planet Earth.
- It was never modeled for them.
- They are not convinced it will really help you, nor have volunteers asked for a written ministry outline.
- Some leaders don't have a clear ministry description for their own role and assignment. They are also trying to figure out what expectations their leaders have for them.
  (Please don't be critical of your leaders.)

Sample Volunteer Ministry Outline
"Small Group Facilitator"

Qualifications:
- Have attended a small group for one year.
- Recommended by another small group leader.
- Able to host 10-15 people in your home.
- Attend monthly facilitator training sessions.

Responsibilities (General Overview):
Host up to 15 people in your home, providing an atmosphere of love and care for those who choose to attend.

Specific Responsibilities:
- Serve coffee and water; soda is optional.
- Provide a safe, quiet, and clean environment.
- Encourage and allow everyone to participate in prepared discussions.
- Follow the outlined materials.

Relationships:
- Report to the area small groups director.
- Recruit and recommend your replacement.

plete the task. (Any leader should love hearing those words.) Begin the development of a ministry outline by laying the groundwork for clear, concise, and succinct information. You are really trying to say, "Don't just tell me I am the right person for this job without answering these important questions." Quietly ask your leader the following basic questions related to qualifications, responsibilities, and relationships:

- What is the area of ministry?
- What do I need to know before I jump into this volunteer role?
- What spiritual gifts, talents, or skills do you think I should have to do this job?

- When do you want me to show up and when do you want this task done? (Note: if the leader says, "Anytime," be sure to challenge and clarify that open-ended time frame.)
- Is there any special training you want me to go through before I begin this role?
- Can you give me in one sentence what it is you want me to do?
- Beyond that one sentence, are there two, three, or four very specific tasks you want me to do?
- To whom do you want me to report or answer to when I am finished with the task or if I encounter a problem?
- Who else will be serving with me?

Sample Volunteer Ministry Outline
"Lawn Care Support"

Qualifications:
- Be in good physical health.
- Enjoy being outdoors in all types of weather.
- Be available from April 1–November 15.

Responsibilities:
- Assist the custodian with outdoor maintenance to bring beauty or order to our property's landscape.
- Be willing to perform any of the following functions with a team spirit.

Specifically:
- Lawn mowing and edging
- Fertilization and weed control (pulling)
- Tree and shrub trimming
- Grounds sweeping (includes parking lot)

Relationships:
- Report to the ministry's chief custodian.
- Work with other volunteers.

- Am I going to be responsible for other people's performance or just my own work?

Do I really expect you to meet with your leader and ask these 10 questions? Yes! They are very important questions, and the answers

---

Ministry Outline Worksheet
Responses to the 10 questions to my leader

Area of Ministry and Title
1. _____

Qualifications:
2. I need to know _____
3. A gift, talent, or skill that I need _____
4. The amount of time expected of me _____
5. Education or training needed _____

Responsibilities:
6. Generally, I am responsible for (big picture overview in one or two sentences)

_____

_____

_____

Specifically, I will:
7. (List two, three, or four specific responsibilities you need to do to meet the overall job expectation as stated in #6 above)

_____

_____

_____

Relationships:
8. I will report to _____
9. I will work with _____
10. I am responsible for _____

will bring clarity and passion for the ministry. I believe the outcomes will be very positive for you and the leader.

Organize the Answers.

The answers to the above ten questions will form the outline for your volunteer ministry description. Questions 1-5 relate to your qualifications to enter the job and be successful. Questions 6-7 address the specific responsibilities and expectations of the leadership. The last three questions, 8-10, outline who you will relate to as you begin your work and service.

Fit your answers into the format titled, "Ministry Outline Worksheet" on page 77. Once you have filled in the answers on the worksheet, go back over your responses. As you review the answers in the worksheet, attempt to model one of the three ministry outline examples in this chapter. Present it to your ministry leader. As you address each question and answer (expectations), remember to keep your conclusions short and simple. Always leave some room for creativity and the unexpected. But address the expectations that will result in joy and ministry satisfaction.

Get the Word Out

A job outline can become a tool of encouragement, unity, and comfort. The document should be circulated to as many people as possible. When a spouse or good friend sees your job outline, they will have a clear understanding of your role. In addition, they will know how to encourage you, pray for you, and possibly join you in the ministry.

A clearly written ministry outline will provide a sense of unity among the leaders and other volunteers. Ministry outlines should be available for any and all to see. The board of directors would do well to have all of the ministry outlines in their community handbook or board notebook.

Let's serve as volunteers with clarity and intentionality, leaving room for creativity and growing passions. Serving Jesus Christ is the greatest of all joys. Serving with other believers in a spirit of support and unity will make our service to Christ even better.

Survey Results

From question #8 in the survey (see Appendix 1):
    59% indicated they had received a ministry outline.
    41% indicated they had not received a ministry outline.

When asked the second part of the question:
    61% indicated a desire to have a ministry outline.
    6% indicated no desire for a ministry outline.
    17% indicated that a ministry outline was not necessary.
    16% did not answer the question.

Insight: While it is clear that the majority of volunteers appreciate and already have a ministry outline for their role, it is obvious that not every role requires a written set of qualifications, responsibilities, and more. Some volunteer roles are that simple, and it is not always necessary to provide a written set of expectations or requirements for every volunteer. However, if you are volunteering and discover that written guidelines and expectations would be helpful, ask your leader to work with you and provide that outline.

From question #5 in the survey:
    26% indicated they volunteer fewer than 2 hours per week.
    26% indicated they volunteer 2-3 hours per week.
    28% indicated they volunteer 3-5 hours per week.
    20% indicated they volunteer more than 5 hours per week.

Insight: It is obvious that not everyone can give the same time commitment for volunteer service. It is also amazing to learn in the second part of this survey question that more than 70 percent of the surveyed volunteers indicated they would give up their career and volunteer full-time if finances were not an issue. My initial response is "Wow!"

Chapter 6

Asking Permission

I believe God rules all by his divine providence
and that the stars by his permission are instruments.
(William Lilly)

Problems are solved on the spot, as soon as they arise.
No front-line employee has to wait for a supervisor's permission.
(Jan Carlzon)

I will never forget two couples who stopped by my office for a visit when I was responsible for the adult education ministry at our church. The couples were respected friends and marvelous volunteers at our growing suburban church. Out of respect for me, their love for the people at the church, and their personal investment of time and energy in several areas of ministry, they stopped by to share they were all planning to leave the church.

I was shocked by their surprise announcement. As I listened, they shared how they had each grown up in small churches and desired to recapture the small-town values for their children. They shared stories of how they participated as families and young children in the worship services and major programs or holiday "productions" at their quaint ethnic, community-based churches. Each one had a tender and meaningful story. Their proposed 15-minute meeting with me lasted well over an hour.

Permission to Serve

We concluded our time in agreement that what they deeply longed to have happen would not happen in our mega congregation. However, we stumbled onto a new idea. I asked them several questions. What if you created a small church within our larger church? What if you imitated the country experience in a specially designed format for yourselves and other families? Would you be willing to find three other couples who feel the same way you do? Would you be willing to come back with a plan to create this new ministry?

We scheduled a second meeting in my office for about six weeks later. The original two couples had committed to come back with at least six other friends to discuss a variety of options. On the evening of that second meeting we needed to find another room as nearly twenty people gathered to talk about the idea of creating a "small church" within a church. The conversation was lively and stimulating. Everyone was excited and more than willing to volunteer and take part in the new venture.

Six more weeks passed by and the new little community church was born inside the walls of a modern high-tech ministry, growing with thousands of members and attendees. The ministry needed no church staff, no funds, and had no other requirements. The volunteer couples did it all. Within two years they were averaging more than a hundred people, and they created a second small church. The spirit was contagious in creating a third group and each year they had their own Christmas pageants and camping program. It was a huge success, and they did it all.

> ### Permission
>
> "Permission" is from the Latin *per-* + *mittere* which means "to allow" or "to give up."

The first two couples never realized they could ask permission to create a ministry unique to their needs and interests. Little did they know the staff and church board would be eager to embrace a new type of ministry that would touch the lives of hundreds of people over the next five years. Their original need turned into a dream that soon became a reality and an exciting adventure. We all learned so much about giving people permission to serve as God leads into new areas of ministry.

What is Permission?

Permission can be an unpopular concept. Some leaders are not warm to the risky idea of granting permission, giving up control, or allowing unfettered freedoms to individuals within or outside an organization. Parents are afraid to give permission to their children. Superpower leaders avoid giving to other nations unbridled access (permission) to anything that would threaten their security. People do not like to lose control of responsibility.

Permission is giving up my personal control. Permission is allowing you freedom to explore and make discoveries on your own. Permission is all about granting you a green light to move forward with me. It says, "I trust you. I believe in you." It also says, "I will be here if you fail and need my help anytime, anywhere, for anything. We are here to rely on each other for everything."

God grants permission to His children to live out His expectations, commands, and mission with a great deal of personal choice and freedom. While God is in control, He does not exercise absolute command and power over every decision we make. God gives us the capacity to choose and exercise a free will to follow Jesus and obey God. When we do, we exercise our love, honor, trust, and respect for God. We then experience His blessings and the fruit of His Spirit. Of course, when we step outside the moral will and plan of God, there are certain consequences we will surely experience as we exercise our selfish freedoms and immoral choices.

Trust is... *"A relationship of reliance"*

Questions:
- Can I rely on you to keep your word?
- Can I rely on you to hold a confidence?
- Can I rely on you to move this ministry forward and not in a direction that is driven by your personal agenda?
- Can I rely on you to be faithful to our code of virtues, according to the Bible?

An old quote that helps build a permission- based culture: "The best way to make a man trustworthy is to trust him."

Permission in Ministry?

When there is love and respect for leadership, the mission, and one another, permission can be a powerful tool in growing or developing a ministry. If a leader can trust his or her volunteers, permission will most often be granted. Just as when children are trusted by their parents, certain freedoms are given and allowances are enjoyed. Most often, the same can be experienced in ministry.

I believe permission in ministry is asking leadership for opportunity and freedom to explore new horizons within the boundaries and mission of the ministry. It is the missional mindset to go where others have not gone. (Read again the Luke 10 passage referred to in chapter 5.) Because of certain time, financial, and personnel restrictions some ministries become hampered in their ability to explore and grow beyond their historic traditions and meaningless routines—the Bible refers to this as vain repetitions. (Of course, some traditions should be protected and valued.)

Ministries that seek new vistas are ministries that grow. In the business world they call it "R and D" (Research and Development). Spying out the Promised Land is a biblical example that became a blessing to all the nations. "Same-ol' Same-ol'" will just not get us there. Every ministry needs explorers, barbarians, and adventurers who will go ahead of the rest of us. They need permission to do that.

Not every leader has the exploration mindset or adventuresome spirit. That is a good thing. If every leader were always looking for new hills to conquer, there would be no home support to sustain the conquests. However, there are some volunteers who are reading this paragraph who are just such adventuresome volunteers. If you are, be an Esther, a Ruth, a Joshua, or a Caleb and seek permission to explore new "lands" and bring back the good news to the others in the ministry.

Here are a few ways you can be an explorer:

- Find new educational materials that have been recently released.
- Visit other dynamic ministries through the Web or with a personal visit and bring back new ideas. You may find that you need only some cosmetic changes or, perhaps, program development.
- Invite outsiders to come into your ministry to make objective observations and insights.

- Spend time with a pad and paper, asking God to inspire your thoughts on how to further enhance the ministry where you serve.

Restriction in Ministry?

I believe restriction in ministry is antithetical to what ministry is all about. If God is the head of the ministry (see Colossians 1:17, 18), we should not place human restrictions on what God may desire to do. I am not talking about boundaries. Boundaries are those God-given safeguards for our protection and the security of others.

However, manmade restrictions need to be checked. Are the restrictions there for personal control? Do they exist because of a low view of volunteers and an inability to trust people? Are they created out of unwarranted fears? If so, the volunteer has a responsibility to ask some good questions and create a dialogue that may or may not reduce some old restrictions that once were valuable but are no longer needed.

How Does One Get Permission?

Begin with demonstrating genuine respect and honor for your leader. While much was said in chapter 1 about establishing a healthy relationship with your leader, this is the place to begin a permission-based ministry.

It is out of respect and honor that one is trusted. Every time you keep a promise and do what you said you would do, you earn

---

Volunteer Guidelines for Asking Permission

- Start with the organization's mission statement, not your own.
- Align your new idea with the ministry's mission and vision.
- Incorporate the ministry's core values and future goals.
- Don't ask for money.
- Don't ask for staff assistance, just permission.
- Don't place other demands on the organization.
- Present a clear, complete action plan that you and others will be able to embrace.

trust. When you show integrity and bring others into the core values of the ministry, you earn trust. When you demonstrate dignity and courtesy to other volunteers, your leaders will take notice and once again, you earn trust. It is out of your life and ministry "trust account" that leaders will be eager to grant you permission to explore and adventure into new areas of ministry.

Be patient and take your time. Some leaders need more time than others to trust you and reward with permission. Some have been burned in the past by giving permission too early. Some have been duped by those with personal agendas for selfish gain. Time can be one of your best friends. Use the time to be consistent and keep earning trust. Also, use the waiting period to explore every avenue of your new adventure and your desire to move the ministry beyond the current walls. Finally, examine your heart. Check your motives. Let time work for you.

Last, but not least, ask. Ask for permission. Don't assume it. Don't just take it. Don't believe for a moment that it is *better to ask for forgiveness than to ask for permission.* That is an enormous lie. It is not true. It is not a funny quip. It breaks down the very essence of what it means to win respect and earn trust.

In the end, it comes back to respect. You may think you have earned permission, but don't just grab it because you believe it is yours to have. No! Show respect for your leader. Then, every time, ask for permission. With trust and respect, I earnestly believe that asking is receiving.

Permission to Fail

So far, what we are talking about is permission to go on adventures and explore new areas of ministry to people with the good news of Christ's message. That kind of thinking and action assumes great success and a moment of celebration at the end. It carries the thought of bringing back treasures and valuable riches for all to see and share. However, not every new exploration ends that way. Some end in failure.

Erwin Lutzer titled a book, *Failure: the Back Door to Success.* He got it right, at least in principle. The underlying principle is this: We just might fail. If your leader gives you permission to explore, you should also be given permission to fail.

Before you begin your ministry journey into unchartered terri-tory, ask your leadership and other volunteers for the following:

- Freedom to share the rough roads without embarrassment.
- Prayer for every step of your travels.
- A place to land if things get too rough.
- An opportunity to bail out if God shuts the door or if resources do not materialize.
- Acceptance, if you fail, that you bit off more than you could chew.

Have the above discussion. Talk about the potential pitfalls, dangers, and potential hazards. Don't pretend that success is always a must. It may be just the opposite, and you need to have a safe place to return after a difficult, awkward, and uncomfortable landing.

Results of a Permission-based Ministry

As a volunteer, you may read this chapter and the creative wheels in your mind may be turning faster than usual. That may be a good thing. Keep thinking and keep praying for God's clear direction.

As you consider where you will seek permission to grow and expand the ministry, consider the outcomes to your potentially new endorsement and freedom in service. The following can also help you establish more healthy reasons to keep moving forward in your pursuit and ministry advance. Share these results with your leaders and other volunteers. Think permission-based ministry. Allow it to expand your heart and thoughts.

Accountability

Let your leaders know that you desire and respect accountability.

We all need a certain amount of accountability. Healthy ac-countability provides safety and structure for all participants in any community of people. Accountability requires that people remain connected. It constantly asks questions and expects reasonable answers.

Accountability is closely linked to responsibility. The two go hand in hand. When people are given permission to explore new areas of ministry, they are also given responsibility to make decisions and help people grow. The more permission granted, the more responsibility expected, the more accountability is needed.

When my wife Donna and I gave permission (earned) to our teenage daughter, she realized she had more responsibility and that required more accountability. She called us, asking for advice and assistance when she was now responsible for the outcomes more often than when we were in charge and she had less freedom. It significantly increased our communication.

I can think of countless examples in ministry where we have seen the same pattern: Permission > Responsibility > Accountability > Communication

Unity

Let your leaders know that you are committed to the unity of believers in the body of Christ.

I believe there can be greater unity when people are respected and given permission to serve as God leads them. From the principles of growing accountability, noted above, permission-based ministry tends to bring people together. The natural fear is that everyone will become independent and autonomous. But, it's not so. When we are given certain freedom, we need resources and the help of others. That drives us back to those who believed in us, the ones who granted permission.

A new spirit of camaraderie can be born out of permission-based ministry. The bottom line is, "I need you." I need help when I am out there on my own. I need a team, partners, and relationships to function well. Community is essential. Serving together is imperative. The outcome can become a unity that brings joy and delight to me and to God (Psalm 133).

Diversity

Let your leaders know that you believe that greater diversity will strengthen this ministry.

Diversity can mean many things. It can relate to gender, race, age, and preferences. Diversity can be threatening to the comfort zones of some while stimulating new insights and perspectives in others.

A permission-based culture usually strips away the bias and cultural restrictions placed on certain diversity issues. When people are free to make choices and develop a passionate area of ministry, one of the last things they consider is the placement of their own predisposed prejudice or favoritism.

It is within permission-based communities that people will sense freedom as a value and find a place for everyone. It is here that people will grow outside their traditions and preconceived notions toward people who think and live differently.

Simplicity

Let your leaders know that you will strive for simplicity in your area of ministry.

Dr. Ed Dobson, while senior pastor at Calvary Church, wrote the book on simplicity in ministry. In fact the book (no longer in print) was titled, *Simplicity*. The book was Ed's philosophy of ministry, which was played out in his life and leadership role. Ed was a permission-giver and created a culture of permission-based ministry. I know. I was there.

The concept of simplicity does not need a lot of explanation. That is the beauty of it. Keep things simple. Or, to be cute, KISS, *Keep It Simple, Servants*. When someone has permission to do a task or perform a role, the last thing they desire or seek is a way to make the ministry or process complicated. Simplicity overrides any bureaucratic structures and systems among the adventuresome barbarians in search of a new mountain. They will attempt to do everything and anything to accomplish the goal as quickly, easily, inexpensively, and simply as possible.

Growth

Let your leaders know that you believe people and the ministry can grow to maturity.

In a permission-based culture, energy levels are high. In a controlled environment, energy levels are low and apathy sets in, creating atrophy. When energy levels are high, usually all systems are energized and work at higher levels of output. In medicine we might call that increased metabolic activity or high metabolism.

Permission-based volunteers are on a constant search for resources, support, and encouragement. Once permission is granted, the energy starts and never seems to stop until permission is denied. At that point, watch everything come to a screeching halt and all systems begin to shut down. Decline begins; growth vanishes.

Boundaries

Let your leaders know that you will seek their help in establishing community boundaries.

It goes without saying that boundaries are imperative in a permission-giving organization. Unhealthy boundaries create suspicion, natural conflict, fear, and restriction. But healthy boundaries will accelerate your volunteer area of ministry.

Children need boundaries to guard their safety and give them a sense of security to explore the good things in their natural development. Volunteers in ministry need the same security and safety through healthy ministry boundaries. As a volunteer, suggest to your leadership where you need some safeguards and safety nets. Don't shy away from requesting simple things to protect you and the people you serve.

Greater Focus on the Mission

Let your leaders know that you are committed to the mission of this ministry.

Every ministry needs constant reminders about how to fulfill the mission rather than how to fill our programs. Wise and mature

---

Volunteer Boundaries

- I will be honest in all of my interactions with people.
- I will not engage ministry plans without seeking approval from the respective board or committee.
- I will not handle ministry funds without an accountability partner.
- I will be discreet in my interactions with people of the opposite sex.
- I will not seek to control other people or speak poorly of this ministry or its leaders.

leadership is not usually looking for one more program to fund, staff, and facilitate unless it will help meet the ministry's mission.

Permission-based ministries can bring significant clarity to the overall mission of any ministry. However, that will depend on you as a volunteer. You can either reinforce the mission or deter away from it. Seeking permission to serve in new arenas should only drive you closer to realizing the ministry's mission, not your own mission.

Survey Results

From question #11 in the survey (see Appendix 1):
> 68% said they were "energized" when given freedom to lead.
> 30% said they were "more cautious" when freedom is given.
> 2% said they were "terrified" to have freedom.

Interestingly, in the second part of question #11:
> 43% indicated "limited boundaries" are preferred.
> 24% wanted "total freedom."
> 14% desired "exact rules" to do their ministry.
> 23% did not respond to this question (the most non-respondents in the survey).

From survey question #14, about 22% indicated they found courage in ministry when freedom was given to them in their area of ministry service.

From survey question #15, volunteers were asked about their opportunity for creativity.
> 59% indicated they "often" feel the freedom to be creative.
> 30% indicated they are "occasionally" allowed to be creative.
> 6% indicated they are "seldom" allowed to be creative.
> 4% never had the opportunity to be creative.

In the second half of question #15 the volunteer's response to routine was questioned. It was evenly expressed by volunteers that routine is needed, enjoyed, or accepted. With the accepted respect for some routine, there seems to be a general interest that volunteers like to explore creative avenues of ministry. Overall, the survey seems to give no indication that any significant percentage of volunteers enjoy serving the status quo.

Insight: Not everyone is wired to be creative or footloose and fancy free. While many people need higher levels of structure than others, most volunteers indicated they want to be trusted and given opportunity to move forward in ministry without major constraints.

When volunteers were asked how they felt about being "micro-managed" (survey question #12b), most of the volunteers surveyed did not respond well. Words shared included: "angry," "captive," "caged-in," "incomplete," "pressured," "confused," "boxed-in," "limited," "bothered," "frustrated," "not empowered," "crowded," "irritated," "inferior," "misunderstood," "trapped," "smothered," "mistrusted," "unnecessary," "watched," "undervalued," "belittled," "controlled," "stalked," "contained," "incompetent," "not needed," "anxious," "catastrophe," "overwhelmed," "minimized," "inadequate," and one of my favorite responses, "ugh." (This was the question in the survey where the greatest variety of words and thoughts were shared in response.)

Very few volunteers (about 8%) indicated they were "Okay" or "Fine" with being micro-managed, making personal footnotes that they were "followers and not leaders."

Question: What are the boundaries that you feel you need for growing in your ministry, and are you willing to share those with your leader?

Chapter 7

Ministry Training and Discovering Your Spiritual Gift

Whatever you have learned or received or heard from me, or seen in me—put it into practice. And the God of peace will be with you.
(Philippians 4:9)

Follow my example, as I follow the example of Christ.
(1 Corinthians 11:1)

Do not neglect your gift, …Be diligent in these matters; give yourself wholly to them, so that everyone may see your progress. Watch your life and doctrine closely. Persevere in them, because if you do, you will save both yourself and your hearers.
(1 Timothy 4:14-16)

It was he [Jesus] who gave some to be apostles, some to be prophets, some to be evangelists, and some to be pastors and teachers, to prepare God's people for works of service, so that the body of Christ may be built up until we all reach unity in the faith and in the knowledge of the Son of God and become mature, attaining to the whole measure of the fullness of Christ. Then we will no longer be infants, tossed back and forth by the waves, and blown here and there by every wind of teaching and by the cunning and craftiness of men in their deceitful scheming. Instead, speaking the truth in love, we will in all things grow up into him who is the

Head, that is, Christ. From him the whole body, joined and held
together by every supporting ligament, grows and builds itself up in
love, as each part does its work.
(Ephesians 4:11-16)

Prepare saints to do what saints are supposed to do.
*(Dallas Willard at the Fellowship of
Evangelical Seminary Presidents, 2004)*

If you read anything in this chapter, read the above wisdom from
God. Underline some of the key verbs. Notice the basic framework
for ministry preparation. It involves three main areas:
Godly Living, Biblical Knowledge, and Spiritual Gifts.

Dallas, Texas, was the location for the annual leadership training
conference for ministry leaders. The conference was geared toward
full-time ministry staff members from various large churches across
North America. It had a reputation for more than 25 years as a major
event with well-known speakers and authors. Directors of adult education, women's ministry directors, and other ministers with adults
made this an annual event on their calendars. They would not miss
it. Neither did eight volunteers from our church.

When the eight men and women approached me about getting
some serious ministry training to be better servants and leaders in
the church's adult ministries, I suggested they attend this conference.
They asked if I was planning to join them. When I looked at my
calendar, I had to send them without me, which turned out to be the
best thing that could have happened.

They attended the four-day training event. When they came
back, here is what I heard: "You did not tell us this was for full-time
clergy." "We were the only volunteers in the entire place." "We started
connecting and learning as if we were ministry staff members." "This
was the best conference we ever attended." "We had a ball."

These eight volunteers wanted the best training available. They
took the initiative. They received the highest level of ministry training available for leaders in adult ministries. They returned with a
bold new leadership capacity that caused them to mature and grow

faster than ever before. (We ultimately hired three of the eight for our staff in about three years.)

As a volunteer, *you must take personal responsibility for your training*. It may be clear to you what you *want to do* in ministry, but the question is, "Are you *prepared and ready* to do it?" Before we begin the preparation process, there is one reality that may need to be embraced. Sometimes the ministry organization in which you serve is not prepared to offer a formal training program. Other ministry demands and priorities keep leadership too busy to create training venues. Many times it is just one added stress on an already underfunded busy program with an already overworked staff. In fact, your ministry leader may have asked you to read this book as an encouragement to begin your self-guided training program.

> ## A Word to the Volunteer
>
> Recognize that training is hard work.
>
> Excellence in training takes many hours over a long period of time.
>
> The best training is not just a curriculum or a system, but a godly person who has been there and done that and understands your questions.

The good news is that volunteer training happens best within the community of believers as the body "builds itself up in love, as each part does its work" (Eph. 4:16). It is in this spiritual community where ministry preparation begins. We are in this together. It is not distance learning. It is hands-on, upfront, and personal encounters with godly people and the God of the Bible. Navigate your training and preparation in ministry with other volunteers.

The three main areas of personal pursuit in preparation for more effective ministry within Christ's body are:

- Godly living: Imitate the spiritual life of a mature believer, who imitates Jesus Christ.
- Biblical knowledge: Learn all that you can about the story of God in the Bible.
- Spiritual gifts: Discover your spiritual gift and your passion for a particular group of people.

Godly Living

A Godly Example

It is essential to find and imitate the spiritual life of a mature believer.

The apostle Paul, who claimed to be the worst of sinners, (a powerful and amazing statement), invites other believers to imitate his example of living the Christian life (1 Cor. 11:1). However, Paul knew the one major condition. He goes on to say, "…as I follow the example of Christ." As Paul imitated the life of Jesus, he gave us an excellent example of how to live like Jesus. As a volunteer, it is our responsibility to show Jesus to others, not just our talents, gifts, and accomplishments.

Our individual personality may be warm, winsome, strong, and engaging, but we are to model Jesus, not any other. In order to follow Jesus, it is good to do two things:

1. Read the Bible and learn everything you can about Jesus (start with the first four books of the New Testament: Matthew, Mark, Luke, and John). Begin thinking and acting like Jesus, one day and one step at a time.

2. Identify a faithful, godly Christ-follower and imitate his or her life in Jesus. How do I find that kind of godly person? Vernon Grounds said it well, "Godliness is the quality of my life that when others look at me, they begin to think of God." Ask God to guide you and look for one person who makes you think about God. When you find that person, pray and seek a way to spend time with her or him.

Ministry's First Steps

Paul challenged his young protégé Timothy toward the pursuit of godliness rather than the pursuit of significance through achievements or relationships.

> But you, man of God, flee from all this, and pursue *righteousness, godliness, faith, love, endurance,* and *gentleness*" (1 Tim. 6:11, emphasis added).

> Fight the good fight of the faith. …I charge you to keep this command without spot or blame *until* the appearing of our Lord Jesus Christ (1 Tim. 6:13-14).

While this appears as a tall order from the Bible, it is not impossible. If it were, God would not have encouraged us to consider these instructions from the apostle. Here are a few things to consider as you begin your journey as an imitator and follower of Christ:

- Ask a leader to help you understand the italicized words in the Bible passage above.

- Make pursuing one of the words in those verses a goal in your life over the next thirty days. Pray and find more verses in the Bible that will help you understand that characteristic of a godly life. After you embrace that quality go to the next one.

- Ask someone to share this journey with you and hold each other accountable. Share with each other little ways this text is making a difference in your lives and ministries.

Speaker, author, and professor Dr. Scot McNight challenged about 100 men and women preparing for ministry: "People will follow you in ministry because of the quality and integrity in your spiritual life, not because of what you know or what you have accomplished." That clearly means character is more significant than competency. Training for ministry begins with personal spiritual growth and development.

A Ministry Mentor

Identify a ministry mentor. Look for people who imitate Jesus Christ. Such a person may be in your ministry. He or she may have been there for a long time, or have just arrived. Ask others in the ministry to point you to spiritually mature people. Ask God to guide you to a person who will encourage you in your spiritual growth and ministry.

Look for someone who reflects the heart of God and the character of Jesus, as you best understand that from the New Testament. If it is someone you have observed and he or she makes you think about God, you may have found your spiritual mentor.

A Spiritual Workout Program

Learn from your mentor. What can your mentor teach you? What is it about his or her everyday life that can become contagious and help

---

Characteristics of Ministry Mentors

- They show an obvious love for God and people.
- The Bible is a book they read and love.
- Prayer is an automatic response to people's needs.
- People are more important to them than programs.
- Ministry obstacles are spiritual challenges for them.
- They know and care about you.

---

you grow? There is only one way to discover those spiritual qualities and characteristics. Ask!

One of the characteristics of a Christ follower is humility (read Phil. 2; 1 Peter 3:8; 5:5). Spiritually mature people are not apt to start talking about themselves. So, ask your mentor the following questions (consider one or maybe two at a time, but resist asking everything in one setting):

- Would you share with me your spiritual journey from the beginning?
- What does Jesus Christ mean to you?
- How do you spend time in the Bible?
- When do you pray? Have you ever fasted?
- What is your ministry and how did you arrive at that role?
- What are your spiritual goals for your life?
- What are your spiritual struggles and how do you plan to find victory?
- What advice or spiritual challenge do you have for me?

Finding and sharing your journey with a spiritual mentor is a privilege. It is not common among people in ministry. However, if you want to accelerate your spiritual growth, learn from someone who knows God and has already traveled the Jesus road.

This level of training is deep and personal. It may last the rest of your life. I hope it does. Beware, you will change. Someone said, "Everything that grows, changes." Be prepared to have your whole heart and your whole life stretched and challenged. Then be prepared

---

A Simple Way to Study the Bible

- Read the same text several days in a row.
- Read the text in more than one version.
- Outline the text in a grammatical outline and underline key verbs and nouns.
- Ask the question, "What is the big idea in this text?" Or "What is the main lesson?"
- Rewrite the text in your own words.
- Check your work by reading a commentary on the same passage.
- Study with a friend and compare insights.

---

to give God praise for the growth in your life and the results of impacting people more deeply in ministry and in life.

Biblical Knowledge

It is important to know how to find biblical truths and principles for ministry.

Read the Bible.

Study two or three key passages in the Bible that you can use in ministry. Ask a leader or mentor for a suggested place to begin your reading. Take your time and learn from God about ministry.

What in the Bible Do I Need to Know to Help Others?

- How to bring someone into a personal relationship with the God of the Bible through Jesus Christ
- How to help a new believer grow in his new found faith
- How to encourage people through tough times
- What the Bible says about prayer, Jesus, the Holy Spirit, and God the Father
- The basics of what it means to follow Jesus as His child and servant
- How to guide yourself or others to find victory over sin and temptation

---

Discover Truth for Learning.

Identify four or five non-negotiable biblical truths for your life and the lives of others.

Commit a key verse to memory as a guide to your daily life and relationship with God. Proverbs 3:5, 6 would be a great place to begin.

Spiritual Gifts

Learn about Spiritual Gifts.

God has given His church spiritual gifts to fulfill His mission. These wonderful God-given gifts are not designed for our personal needs but for the needs of others. I do not have the gift of leadership to enjoy being a leader but to obey God when He places my life into a leadership role or responsibility. Here are a few points to consider as you explore your spiritual gift(s):

- Every believer has a spiritual gift to encourage and impact other people (1 Cor. 12:7).
- We do not choose our own spiritual gift(s); they are given to us by God's Spirit (1 Cor. 12:11).
- We are not all given the same gift (Rom. 12:6).
- We are encouraged to use our gifts to serve others, not ourselves (1 Peter 4:10).
- God's picture of how we should relate to each other is like the parts of our body. Though separate and unique, we need each other and must serve each other (1 Cor. 12:12-31).
- The context of using our gift is in a loving relationship with people (1 Cor. 13:1-13).
- Any gift can be used to impact any people group regardless of age, race, or gender.

Understand the Spiritual Gifts.

The most familiar verses in the Bible that list various spiritual gifts are Romans 12:3-8, 1 Corinthians 12:1-31, Ephesians 4:7-13, and 1 Peter 4:7-11. Nearly twenty spiritual gifts are mentioned in these Bible passages. The first step in discovering your gift begins with a clearer understanding of what God has to say about specific gifts. I have attempted simply to describe the ten most common gifts that volunteers use while they serve and impact the lives of others. These definitions and examples of various areas of ministry service can be an initial study to guide you in your journey.

GIFT	DEFINITION *The supernatural ability and responsibility to:*	EXAMPLES of SERVICE
Shepherding/ Pastoring	...feed, protect, and care for long-term spiritual needs of individuals or groups in the body of Christ, enabling them to grow toward spiritual maturity (The word "pastor" is used only in Eph. 4:11.)	Sunday School leader Counseling Elder Small groups
Teaching	...clearly and accurately communicate the truths of the Bible in such a way that people learn (1 Cor. 12:28, 29; Eph. 4:11)	Any teaching role Discipleship
Evangelizing	...effectively communicate the good news of Jesus Christ (Acts 21:8; 2 Tim. 4:5)	Outreach Teaching
Exhorting	...come alongside and provide encouragement, strength, stability, consolation, help, and to bring course correction to another (Rom. 12:8)	Counseling Discipleship People support
Mercy	...show great empathy and compassion for those who suffer physically, emotionally, or spiritually, and to assist them in their need without judgment (Rom. 12:8)	Visitation Prayer ministry Personal care Ministry to the poor

Helping/ Serving	...unselfishly meet the needs of others, freeing them to exercise their spiritual gift(s) to meet others' needs (1 Cor. 12:28; Rom. 12:7)	Any support Maintenance Secondary role Behind the scenes
Giving	...give freely, cheerfully, and sacrificially of one's resources for the sake of Christ and His body	Outreach Greeting Special needs
Administering	...provide leadership in the organization and direction for the goals of the body of Christ by designing and carrying out an efficient plan of action (General concept: moving other people toward stated objectives, Rom. 12:8)	Boards Committees Start or manage ministries
Faith	...confidently determine the will and purpose of God for His work and to believe that God will accomplish it, even when it looks impossible (1 Cor. 12:9)	Leadership team Ministry support Prayer ministry

Other spiritual gifts include apostleship, discernment, knowledge, prophecy, wisdom, and several sign gifts, which are for the purpose of making Christ known (1 Corinthians 14:22). Your gift is God's good gift to you. More than anything else, it is given to you to define and design your specific role in ministry.

Get involved in Ministry.

Go ahead; jump into the deep end. Get involved in people's lives. Find an entry point of service and share your life and the goodness of God with others. Experiment and try various areas of service.

Seek Feedback.

If the framework for using our spiritual gifts is the body of Christ and love for others, it is important to listen to people who have been

---

How to Identify Spiritual Gift Coaches

- They know their spiritual gift.
- They desire to encourage you.
- They can observe you in a variety of ministry and life roles.
- They will commit to pray for you.
- They will give you positive and honest feedback on what may or may not be your gift.
- Together, you will not rush in the process of discovering your gift from God.

---

a part of your life and ministry. You need to hear their response to your involvement in their lives. Here are a few things to consider:

- What do people say you have done to minister to them? Listen for the gifts of God's Spirit to be made known through this ministry.
- Why do people come to you? Is it for help, mercy, leadership, shepherding, or ___?
- Do any of the gifts listed above describe your role in their lives?

As you listen to others, there should be some significant indicators of God's design for your life and ministry. Pay attention and respect what others say.

Look for Holy Spirit Confirmation.

Allow God to confirm your gift by His Spirit. After understanding the definitions of spiritual gifts, involving your life in ministry, and listening to God's people respond to your ministry in their lives, it is time to reflect, asking God to make His role in ministry very clear to you. Spend time in reflection and prayer. Give it some time. Clarity by God's Spirit will bring a new sense of confidence and fulfillment as you serve God and others. Then rejoice in God's leading in your life.

Consider Your Uniqueness.

What Is Your Passion? Each gift may be used in almost every age group ministry whether children, youth, or adult. The application of

Build Your Own Ministry Tool Kit by Asking:

- Where do I need to grow?
- What weaknesses do I need to overcome?
- Am I confident of my spiritual gift?
- What personal spiritual disciplines need strengthening?
- What people skills can I better develop?
- What are my leadership and learning styles?
- What material do I need to read to do this ministry to the glory of God?
- Who can I identify as a ministry model?
- Where is this ministry being done best?

Answers to these questions will give you a powerful set of tools (resources) to grow and develop your God-given ministry.

your spiritual gift is not determined by gender, age, or background. It is God's good gift to you to minister to others.

A significant part of your training process is to identify your "mission field." That answers the question, "To whom has God called me to share my life, gifts, talents, and His love and grace?"

If we believe that ministry is about people, then our passion must be people. Passion is not about feelings as much as it is about a commitment to a particular people. For example, if my passion is for teenagers, then they are what I think about, and I desire to see changes in their lives.

To identify your area of passion (people group), answer the following questions:

- Who do I think about the most?
- Who do I find myself going out of my way to help and encourage?
- For whom do I pray the most?
- With whom do I find joy and energy when being involved in ministry?

When you discover your gift and find your passion, ministry begins to come alive!

What Is Your Comfort Zone? Every one of us has a comfort zone. There are three general categories in which we may feel confident and secure:

- One-on-one
- Small groups (3-12 people)
- Large groups (number of people is not a concern)

Simply identify in which of the above arenas you are most comfortable. This is the third component in identifying your strength in ministry.

In summary, your gift + your passion + your comfort zone = your defined area of ministry. Making these three discoveries is a significant outcome in preparing for ministry. Now, the excitement begins. Maybe the commencement to this ministry sounds something familiar like this, "On your mark, get set, go!"

Survey Results

From question #2 in the survey (see Appendix 1):

68% indicated they were confident in knowing their spiritual gift.

28% indicated they had reservations about their spiritual gift.

4% had no clue what gift God had given to them.

Insight: Knowing your spiritual gift is important to volunteers in ministry. However, more than 30%, or one of every three volunteers from our survey, indicated there is a need for additional training to discover their gift with confidence.

Question: How important for effective service is it to know your spiritual gift?

From question #9 in the survey, we note that

40% learned how to do their ministry "on the job" or on their own.

32% learned how to do their ministry through a training program.

28% learned how to do their ministry by watching others, again "on the job."

Insight: Only one of every three volunteers has learned how to do ministry through a training program. It might be reasonable to assume that the same one-third has been offered training through their ministry organization. If not, they have to find their own training program as well as watch others and make their own attempts to learn how to serve. In other words, most volunteers are left to figure out how to do ministry by watching others or simply figuring it out on their own.

Question: What are the strengths and weaknesses of learning ministry without a formal training process?

From question #14 in the survey, 47% of the surveyed volunteers said that through training they found courage to move forward in ministry.

Insight: Training is a highly perceived value in the volunteer's ministry role. If it is a source of courage to nearly one of every two volunteers, then volunteers would do well to find or take advantage of training opportunities.

Chapter 8

Finding Resources to Get the Job Done

Suppose one of you wants to build a tower.
Will he not first sit down and estimate the cost
to see if he has enough money to complete it?
For if he lays the foundation and is not able to finish it,
everyone who sees it will ridicule him, saying,
"This fellow began to build and was not able to finish."
(Luke 14:28-30)

For the Scripture says, "Do not muzzle the ox while it is treading
out the grain," and "The worker deserves his wages."
*(1 Timothy 5:18, quoted by the apostle Paul from Deuteronomy 25:4
and the words of Jesus to the 72 volunteers in Luke 10:7.)*

There is little question among Bible scholars that the verse above refers primarily to financial remuneration for those who serve in ministry. The biblical text flows in a context of providing monetary resources for widows and orphans. Were all elders in this first century church on the ministry's payroll? We can assume that some were and some were not. Regardless of their remuneration, the principle here is that the church is to take care of those who engage in ministry. The church is encouraged to provide material resources to avoid creating unnecessary financial burdens for those who serve.

An Example

Darlene was a volunteer in her church. She was charged to design and develop a new curriculum for the adult discipleship program. After Darlene agreed to fully immerse her life in this great task, she was notified there would be no funds available to purchase printed curriculum.

Instead of complaining or resigning, Darlene asked for a few other resources. She asked for access to the church computers, printers, and copy machines. She asked that the church purchase paper, staples, and other basic products so she could begin writing and assembling her own study materials.

Darlene used every creative resource available. She read other curriculum materials. Surveys were conducted among many adults in the church community. Darlene began to collate all the soft resources of information and to create a brand new discipleship guide for the women and men in her church. It was a great success and cost very little. But, she had the tools to develop the curriculum.

Resources are more than money. Darlene proved that well. Resources to get the job done may include people, time, space, reputation of the ministry, communication, decision-making, networking with other ministries, use of physical equipment, and of course, funds. It is always best to ask for resources. Never assume that you are

---

How Volunteers Recruit Other Volunteers

Step One: Share your ministry with a friend.

Step Two: Invite a future volunteer to join you in watching and observing your ministry role.

Step Three: Ask the future volunteer for her reflections and feedback on the ministry.

Step Four: Ask the new recruit to pray about joining you in a specific role.

Step Five: Write a very simple Ministry Outline (see chapter five).

Step Six: Ask for a trial involvement with time for review and a final longer-term commitment.

entitled to resources of the parent ministry because of your longevity or status in the ministry community. It is also wise to remember that some leaders do not always know what it takes to complete a particular task or ministry outcome. Don't be shy. Make your needs known. Be a wise builder by counting the cost and securing all of the finest available resources. Consider the following resources as needed for effective ministry.

"Hard" Resources

Human Resources

Sometimes you just need more help (most of the time?). More help means recruiting more volunteers to come alongside you to shoulder the task. No one can recruit someone in your area of ministry better than you. You intimately know what is needed and who will be the best fit in the ministry.

As you prepare to take action steps to recruit friends and others seeking to be engaged in the ministry with you, be sure to:

Clearly articulate the vision.
Not everyone knows your area of ministry. Consider how to define what is happening in your place of service. Write it down. Take the eraser out and get it down to as few words as possible. If you can share the vision from the first floor to the third floor in an elevator, then you know you've articulated your vision with clarity and conviction.

Identify your needed workforce.
As a wise builder, attempt to figure out how many people will be needed to develop or manage this ministry. Luke 14:31, 32 paints a powerful picture of a king going into battle. If he does not have enough soldiers to win the battle, he looks for terms of peace. In other words, he surrenders and does not engage in the war. Paul describes ministry a bit like going into battle (Eph. 6). As a volunteer, be sure to find out if you have enough human resources. If not, one of two things will happen. You will either do it all yourself and potentially become a casualty, or you will need to surrender to the "enemy." Count the cost.

Establish ministry-minded relationships.
Begin now to identify people who share the same biblical core values, passion, and missional outcomes. Develop a friendship and ongoing dialogue about God's activity in your community and outside your walls. Build those relationships to the point where you can begin the simple steps of inviting them to join you in what God is doing.

Time

Time has become one of the most expensive commodities in our fast-paced culture. It seems as though we never have enough time. I have often encouraged volunteers with this phrase, "Time is still your best friend." I don't hear God saying, "Hurry up." Timing is most often God's department.

The first thing God encouraged the volunteers in Acts chapter one to do was "wait." God desires that we make the best use of every opportunity He provides for us (Eph. 5:16). We ought to be good stewards. Ask your leader for the time you need to do ministry with all your heart and with excellence. Some leaders get in a hurry (I confess to being one of them) and expect volunteers and staff to go faster and get the job done quicker. You know your pace. "Get it done quickly" is not always the best use of our time. Time is a necessary resource that can lead to excellence, quality, and care in people's lives.

Facilities (space)

Ministry space is always at a premium. Prime space is a point of warfare in many areas of ministry. Many will argue for their wants of convenience, ambience, best location, and more. Try not to get caught up in those petty preferences. Think about the people you serve, especially when the best space is not available. Ask yourself, what space do we need to develop this area of ministry today and what might it be for tomorrow?

Next, request the space needed from your leaders. If they inform you that no space is available, begin a process of creative and blue-sky thinking. Maybe you need to flex on time or consider space in a totally different location. Whatever the outcome, share your need and ask your leader for assistance with an alternative plan from you.

Letter for a Gift-in-Kind

(When you donate an item or professional service, you may request the following short letter from the ministry you serve.)

Current Date

Dear Volunteer (your name),

Thank you for your gift of (service or item) received by this ministry on (date received) with our thanks and appreciation.

Sincerely,

(Officer in the Ministry)

(It is up to you, not the ministry, to establish a dollar value for the professional service or item. Once again, be sure to check with your accountant.)

Equipment

Equipment is expensive. Equipment breaks down, requiring costly repairs and maintenance. Machines, no matter how new, quickly become outdated in our technologically advancing world and throw-away consumerism.

Yet, we cannot seem to get along without those copy machines, collators, electric staplers, computer-driven color printers, postage machines, and the ministry van or bus. While we were promised that all of these modern marvels would make life better, we find ourselves standing in line to get the next job accomplished, and frustrated when the current man-made machine breaks down and we need to accomplish our task "the old way."

As a volunteer, you may need to take the initiative to secure and utilize needed tools and equipment. If your ministry does not have open availability for volunteers to use the equipment at the ministry, depending on the size of your context, ask leaders…

… for a written policy as to who, when, and for what use certain equipment may be used. (Written policies protect you more than hinder you.)

...to add the needed funds to purchase or lease a particular piece of equipment in next year's budget.

...to allow you to purchase and donate a piece of equipment and request a "gift-in-kind" donation letter.

...to establish an account at the local "speedy print" place in town.

...to permit you to shop and get bids on equipment leases, purchases, or shared arrangements with another ministry (network partner in ministry). Sometimes, leaders do not have the time to chase down that kind of detail. Be the first volunteer who offers to get some information.

"Soft" Resources

Reputation

This is considered a "soft" resource. Every ministry has a reputation inside and outside the community. If the reputation of your ministry is positive, leverage it. Use this intrinsic value as a powerful resource to recruit other people. Let the positive name of your ministry open doors to other partnerships and networks outside your walls.

Build on what has already been established. Celebrate and promote the good stories and healthy quality of the existing organization. Invite others to join you in what God has done and what you believe God is yet to do.

Building on your Parent Ministry's Healthy Reputation

- Use the name of your ministry in all your printed materials.
- Invite your ministry leaders to participate if they are respected in the community.
- Hold your ministry event, if possible, at your ministry's location. It is not always a plus to have events off campus unless there is no space available on campus.
- When you are off campus, use the name of your ministry as the sponsor or host of the event.

Create Your Own Ministry Tool Kit

(Complete this outline to create the tools that are necessary for healthy ministry.)

- List your need for additional help.
- Identify the amount of time needed each week to develop a dynamic ministry or to complete your required tasks.
- Note the space that is needed now and what is anticipated for the future.
- What do you need others to know about your ministry? Identify two or three tools to make that information available to others.
- List who you will go to with special requests and concerns.
- Identify who else is doing this ministry in another church, city, or state.
- Make a list of needed equipment you do not currently have available to you.
- Create a real and an ideal budget.

If the ministry's reputation has negative overtones in the community, it is even more important to focus on fostering and sharing the stories of good news. If you don't tell the good stories, others are left to tell the not-so-good stories. So, let's make it a good story!

Communication

In Chapter 4 we discussed the need to communicate what is happening and what is needed in your ministry. Ask for space in existing communication brochures and other written and verbal forms of announcements. Offer to your leader to write what you want people to know. If you are not a writer, ask someone who is a writer to assist you.

Present your communication information in advance. Leaders and people who put communication tools together do not get excited about last-minute information.

Authority

There will be times when a decisive action step needs to be taken. You will not always have the luxury of weeks or months to wait for

---

List of Tax-Deductible Expenses

Be sure to check with your accountant, but the following are often tax-deductible volunteer expenses.

- Mileage for the use of your vehicle from the place of ministry to the event and back
- Actual expenses incurred for the ministry, when requested to do so by leadership, such as gas, food, paper, stamps, books, and more
- Depreciation on certain capital expense items, such as a computer or sound system purchased for the ministry's use

---

a committee or board to convene on an important matter that may have surprised you and others in the ministry process. It is important that you know how decisions are made in your ministry context, especially in emergencies.

You need to know how your leader is empowered to make decisions. While there may be certain decisions that require a board or committee response, many do not. Ask your leader what authority you have to make necessary basic or general decisions to get the job done.

Networking

We discussed the importance of developing an internal partnership in chapter 2. Sometimes you may need to go outside your ministry to find available resources. There are other ministries that have already experienced and accomplished what you are now trying to achieve. Discover who they are and ask for assistance. Request resources from other ministries such as samples of curricula, a copy of their strategic plan, examples of their publications and literature, and other written materials.

Ask for permission to use the resources of others in your ministry, giving credit where credit is due. Another ministry may also be a good place to find equipment resources or shared space. At our seminary, several ministries have used our space and equipment to accomplish their ministry goals. We are always delighted to be asked and to participate.

Funding

Finally, it often takes money to get the job done. While that is not always the case, when it is, there should be a financial plan for needed resources. There are several venues to locate necessary dollars for ministry projects. The most common are:

Budgeted Dollars

These are the funds that the ministry agrees to raise and make available for ministry needs.

Designated Account

This is a board-approved line in the current budget that begins with zero funds available. Volunteers and others may give tax-deductible dollars to this account for ministry use, as overseen by the financial committee or board.

Gifts-in-Kind

These are gifts or professional services that volunteers and outside ministry friends may donate. While the gift is not money, it can be a

---

Sample of a Reimbursement Form

Request that your ministry establish a short form similar to this for reimbursement of your cash expenses for ministry service.

Name of Ministry
Address of Ministry

Your name
Your address
Date of expense(s): _____

- List each expense item (e.g., food, fuel, supplies, etc.):
- Amount of each expense and total:
- Purpose of expense(s):
- People engaged or connected to expense:

*Be sure to attach the actual receipts (not copies) to this form for a cash reimbursement.

receipted gift with a "Gift-in-Kind" letter (See inset on page 111for a sample form.) With a gift-in-kind, the ministry must accept the gift, and the donor must place a value on the gift.

Your Checkbook

As God places on our hearts to give, we need to give. Out of obedience to the Spirit of God prompting us to act, we must surrender our will to the needs of the ministry. Sacrificial giving can prove to be one of the greatest joys of life and ministry.

While the checkbook option may not appear to be the most popular, sometimes it is. When people are engaged wholeheartedly, their treasure seems to follow. We cannot ignore or discount the words of Jesus, "Where your treasure is, there your heart is also" (Matt. 6:21). There is every reason to believe the opposite is true as well: Where your heart is, there your treasure is also. I have watched people fall in love with ministry as God worked in their lives. I have seen their joy and uncounted hours of dedication. I have also seen them give sacrificially out of their financial resources. I have seen them do that cheerfully as to the Lord Jesus. God has seen everything that they have done. That is what matters the most.

Survey Results

In question #10 in the survey (see Appendix 1):
    56% indicated that resources are available.
    34% indicated that resources are minimal.
    10% did not respond to the question.

In the other part of the question
    23% indicated they spent a lot of money as a volunteer.
    55% indicated they covered minor expenses for the ministry.
    22% indicated they spent no money on the ministry.

Insight: While it is virtually impossible to judge the reasons for the above expenses, it is obvious that many volunteers do spend money out of their own pockets for ministry expenses. It appears that providing resources has become a partnership between the ministry and the volunteers. This concept raises some serious questions and should stimulate a healthy dialogue in your ministry.

Questions: To what extent should volunteers financially support the work of the ministry? To what extent should the ministry provide the funding?

Chapter 9

Starting a New Program Through Innovation

Be strong and courageous. Do not be terrified;
do not be discouraged, for the Lord your God
will be with you wherever you go.
(Joshua 1:9)

The body is a unit, though it is made up of many parts;
and though all its parts are many, they form one body. So it is with
Christ. Now the body is not made up of one part but of many.
(1 Corinthians 12:12, 14)

I looked for a man among them who would build up the wall
and stand before me in the gap on behalf of the land
so I would not have to destroy it, but I found none.
(Ezekiel 22:30)

I believe God's desire, more than ever, is for men and women who are willing to "stand in the gap." He calls out to those who are paid staff and volunteers in ministry, "Who will make a difference? Who will do for Me what others are not willing to do?"

Patty is one who stood and filled the gap where there was a huge disparity. That cavernous need was in women's ministry in a city where little was being done to reach out to women who were misunderstood and marginalized.

Patty started as a volunteer. For years she built relationships and established Bible studies for women in her church. Her impact was far reaching and women began to respond with new confidence to the love and grace of God. A ministry was birthed and Patty had to make a choice—lead the ministry, find someone else to lead, or let it go.

She could not let go and no one else was ready to stand in the leadership gap. Patty asked God for wisdom, insight, and courage. She boldly moved forward, confident that God's Spirit would lead her. Did she have all the answers? No. Was she simply a willing servant of Jesus? Yes. She wholeheartedly moved forward in obedience, sacrifice, and surrender.

One by one, women came to faith in Christ. One by one, women started to grow and serve other women. One by one, a variety of ministries were started under this newly born women's ministry. Women started serving young moms, single parents, and women in the community who expressed a hunger to study the Bible. The numbers grew to hundreds of people who were involved. The community was touched and the next step was beyond the American borders to countries in Africa and Central Asia. God was at work, and He started with one person, Patty.

If you met Patty today, you would find a high energy, excited, expressive wife and mother of three adult children. She will still admit to not having all the answers and to be searching for more help, insights, and tools for her ministry toolkit. While she communicates with articulate, persuasive, and loving passion for ministry, she is always asking others to lead and use their God-given gifts. Patty never set out to be a leader. She simply responded with courage and compassion to the special needs of women around her. She initiated what needed to be done, and other women joined her. The church was not the first to call her a leader. It was the participants in the ministry who identified Patty as their leader.

This story is not unusual. In every non-profit ministry you will find volunteer champions like Patty. There are many non-paid men and women with passion and drive, determined to "get the job done." Sometimes, they will step up to the plate, take a swing and strike out. Other times they will hit "grand slams" right out of the park. Regardless of the results, God is using volunteers to begin new initiatives with fervor and zeal. This chapter attempts to give you an encouraging nudge to be one of those ministry champions for a needy group of people in your church, organization, or community.

Be Passionate

Begin with Your Passion and Dream. What has God placed on your heart? Or, a better question, *who* has God placed on your heart? Ministry is about God and people. More specifically, it is about pointing people to the God of the Bible.

For some volunteers, their ministry role and service simply means using their spiritual gift wherever, whenever, with whomever. For others a greater zeal and passion are found when serving a particular people group as well as utilizing their God-given gifts. My good friend and ministry coach Jim Griffith says, "We all should have a mission field."

So, who is your mission field? Who do you think about the most when you consider serving Jesus Christ through His church or the ministry where you are engaged? Is there a particular group of people with whom you relate the best? Do children, teenagers, college students, young adults, middle-aged, or older adults capture your thoughts, heart, and attention? Or, do lost people, those who hurt, lonely people, marginalized individuals, or the people in your neighborhood draw your energy and desire to serve them? You need only one answer to the above questions. That is where you will discover your greatest passion. Remember *passion = people.*

Scott has a wholehearted passion for inner city people. The poor, homeless, marginalized, and disenfranchised people who live on the streets of our city captured the heart of Scott and his wife Amy. Scott found himself walking the inner city streets of his community's roughest neighborhoods, and he began developing trusted friendships with people who had no one in their lives who cared about them. Scott and Amy showed they cared. As their activity increased, God led this young couple to a local urban school where they volunteered on the playground in order to build relationships with children and their families. It took months before the children would trust Scott and Amy with their stories and affections.

Scott and Amy continued creating consistent, faithful friendships. Slowly, mentoring and teaching took place. Before long, they recruited and involved other volunteers from their church and a new ministry was born. Today, The Urban Family Ministry is a stable non-profit ministry to children and families in a fast-growing Midwestern community. It all began as God used the passion and willingness of one couple who cared about and loved one group of people, their mission field.

Be Zealous

Attempt to Get Leadership to Say, "No." It is one thing to have a passion and love for a people group. It is another thing to do something (above and beyond) about it. Zeal is the next step beyond passion. Zeal is that commitment to do what needs to be done out of your passion. In the Bible, King David said, "*...zeal for your house consumes me ... Zeal wears me out*" (Psalm 69:9; 119:139). Zeal is the wholehearted devotion and commitment God is looking for in ministry volunteers.

When I was in Minnesota, I mentored five interns from Bethel Theological Seminary who were involved in the church's youth ministry. As each one was assigned a mission field (age group of students), I challenged them with one important idea, "Get me to say, 'No.'" That was their challenge. You would not believe the wild and crazy ideas that came out of their minds. And the teens loved every one. The interns became consumed with getting to know and loving the young people. They worked long, hard hours and

What Causes Some Capable Volunteers Not to Step Forward and Lead?

- Lack of encouragement
- Absence of permission by leadership
- Little or no vision in the ministry
- Lack of resources
- Previous failure
- Wrong motives
- Negative self-talk that says, "I can't"
- Some leaders make it clear no one else should lead other than paid staff

were nearly worn out by the end of their first year. After two years, the church hired four of them as regular staff, and they are zealous ministry leaders to this day.

Is your ministry driving you to do above and beyond what is expected? Do you think, dream, plan, and talk about the people in your mission field? Do you find yourself spending time, money and energy that you did not think you had—and it doesn't seem to matter? Zeal for God and His ministry is a good thing. It is contagious, and it may just lead to people and places you never dreamed of.

Be Specific

Articulate the Specific Details about the People's Need. No one knows your area of service and ministry better than you. People are often ignored and neglected in an area of ministry because nothing is said about their needs. You may be their only voice. Have you considered that God has placed you in their lives to serve them and represent them to the larger community of believers?

David and Marjorie have volunteered with the differently-abled children and adults in their church for nearly ten years. Their passion and zeal are unparalleled. Talk about people with wholehearted devotion; they are at the top of the list. As they served, they realized the enormous needs not only within the church, but beyond. They went into the community and learned from scores of adult foster care homes that had a need for a community of faith. David presented the need and opportunity to the church board. The board granted permission to establish the ministry.

With a small team of additional volunteers (that they recruited), they began providing transportation and access for the many groups of foster care adults to come to the church. Recently, the church allowed the "choir" from this group to sing in front of the entire church body. Not a dry eye was found as nearly one hundred people with physical and mental disabilities worshiped the God of grace and love. It all started with two people making the need known to the church and community, and now more than 100 have found a new family of God. The differently-abled people now have a voice that is loud and clear. David and Marjorie made a difference.

Be Creative

Creativity is all about being a "Problem-Solver." That is Pastor Leith Anderson's definition of creativity, "problem-solving." Too often we confuse creativity with artistry. The two certainly merge in many areas of life and ministry, but they are separate entities. While we enjoy the artistic touches to a song or painting, we need problem-solvers in ministry. Ministry is not exempt from having problems, issues, and concerns.

Here is where to begin. Find a need and fill it. Okay, I know that sounds like something Robert Schuler or Norman Vincent Peale would say, but it is an important ministry principle. The opposite of the above cliché is to see a need and ignore it. Ministry needs volunteers who will not look in the other direction when there is a need to be addressed.

Second, problem solving is not just talking about the challenge or problem that lies ahead. In Christian ministry, problems require the people of God to take simple (sometimes radical) steps to resolve the problem. Good problem-solvers take the following natural steps:

- Commit initial observations to God in prayer.
- Clearly and objectively observe and identify the concern as a recurring problem or pattern.
- Verify the concern by asking one or two others if they see the same need. (Don't stop here.)
- Continue to pray and consider one or two simple solutions to resolve the concern.
- Gather available resources and list additional resources needed to solve the problem.
- Invite one or two other willing volunteers to join you in sharing the need with the ministry's leadership person or team.
- Volunteer and ask permission to do what needs to be done.
- Keep communicating with everyone involved.

Marian noticed a problem in her ministry context. She was involved in a single adult program for those who had adult children. The majority of the people in the fast-growing group came from a recent

What Causes Some Ministries to Get Stuck in a Rut?

- Lack of focus on God
- Absence of biblical core values
- Lack of vision and clearly defined outcomes
- Lack of leadership
- Unwillingness to dream, discuss, and try new ideas
- Struggles between leaders with unhealthy egos
- Lack of resources
- Non-responsive community leaders toward volunteer initiatives
- Infighting and competition among volunteers

divorce. Some of the widows and widowers could not relate to those who had been through the pain of rejection from a separating spouse. Their pain and loss was different, and the group did not seem to meet their needs. Some of the people who had lost a spouse to death tried the married couples groups in the church, but that did not seem to meet their lonely needs either.

Marian continued to pray and listen to the needs of some of the divorced people. Her passion and concern grew for those who were struggling from the death of their spouse. Some of the needs of the widows and widowers were overwhelming. Marian did not know what to do, but she knew something had to be done. Marian herself was a senior adult, and she had never started or led a ministry before.

She had to do something and she did. She approached the ministry staff at the church and asked for a room, the use of the kitchen, and opportunity to invite speakers to a monthly luncheon to encourage those who had lost a spouse to death. She recruited a small army of volunteer cooks and wait staff and invited people to the first dinner. And then she courageously invited all of the church board members to attend and sit at different tables in order to ask the attendees how they could pray for them. The board members came and were never the same again.

The first dinner was a great success, and eight years later the dinners continue to be a great source of healing and hope for those who have lost their spouse. Other gatherings and ministries were born out of one woman's zealous efforts, and paid staff are not involved. Way to go, Marian! You are creative. (She would say, "No"). You solved a huge problem and met a greater need.

Be Imaginative

Think outside the box and draw on the imaginations of others. God has given us imaginations. It is a gift from God to dream and consider how lives can be changed and how ministry can be established to bring glory to God. It is out of imaginative thinking that new ministries unlike any others are created. It is in the imagining time that one can see others using their spiritual gifts to the glory of God.

Mallory is a young adult. She just graduated from college. During her junior year in college, she took a trip to Haiti, and her heart was broken for the needs of the people she met. The poverty, sickness, and homelessness of children never left her thoughts. She had to make a difference. So instead of just having a meaningful experience, her mind kicked into overtime. All Mallory could think about was the lost children in Haiti.

Mallory made numerous trips to Haiti, each time taking people with her. She began to imagine what it would be like to provide adoption for children who were sick and almost dying. Her thoughts led to action, and after she consulted with attorneys and legal authorities, a new not-for-profit ministry was born. While Mallory has never taken any money for herself, this young super volunteer has worked with hospitals, providing surgery for children and arranging for adoptions. Her imagination does not stop as she continues to dream of what God will do next.

Be Innovative

Don't be afraid of a new idea. Just because it has never been done before does not mean it cannot be done. The word innovation sounds a lot like invention. It begins with identifying a need. That need is then generated in one's heart as a personal quest. That quest demands a plan and the desire to do something about it. Innovation is the plan with action steps.

Often we hear, "Great idea, who is going to do it?" An idea is only as good as the ability to bring it to reality. Ideas may be a dime a dozen, but people who have the industry and drive to bring any one of the dozen ideas to fruition are not a dime a dozen. Innovators are a rare breed in our culture. They have great worth.

> **Innovation is:**
>
> an adaptive response to disruptive threats. It demands a total community response! *(Bob Cooley, 2008)*

If God is leading you to innovate, be the rare and valuable person who steps out and gets things started. There are others waiting for you to take those first steps.

Pastor and former college president Dr. Wilbur Welch is known for the phrase, "*Stop standing staring up the steps and start stepping up the stairs.*" There are a lot of volunteers who are mesmerized staring up some great steps but have no clue or courage how to take that first step. Innovation begins with taking a first step.

Be Inclusive

Ask others to join you. Take people on a bold new adventure with you. Share your excitement for ministry with others. Not everyone reading this chapter is going to be a ministry starter. They need you to lead the charge. They are waiting for your invitation to go where no one else has gone before.

My dad is a ministry volunteer. When he heard about the need and request from a local nursing home for someone to conduct a weekly Bible study, Dad responded. After a few weeks of going solo, he realized he needed help, and he wanted to share his newly found joy. His first recruit was Richard, who had never done anything quite like this before. Before long Dad and Richard were leading singing and teaching the Bible to senior adults. Then they both started inviting others to come to share their personal faith story. Others were invited to sing songs of worship and praise. They even have a volunteer choir from other churches. I have no idea how many people have helped these two faithful volunteers. All I know is on my last visit to Dad in Arizona, I too became a volunteer and taught one of his Bible studies.

Volunteers who do ministry alone will finish ministry the same way, alone. God has called us to serve in community. Being one part of the body reminds us of the importance of each additional part of the body.

Steve Venture in "Start Right…Stay Right" (*Walk the Talk*, Dallas: The Walk the Talk Co., 2004, p. 14) writes, "Of course they [volunteers and initiators] represent more work. So what? Extra effort is what increases your ability to make a difference…to develop, grow, and show what you can do. That's how you separate yourself from the rest of the pack. That's precisely why volunteering and displaying initiative are success factors."

Be an Initiator

Be the one who get things started. Take the first steps toward a new initiative. First of all, develop an action plan. Some readers will have a knee jerk reaction to the words "action plan." However, we all have action plans in our lives whether we realize it or not. We plan for meals that we cook. We plan vacations, events, hobbies, purchases, and visits with friends. We all know how to plan; sometimes we just don't like to do it. Now, there are others who are saying, "Planning is sweet music to my ears." Whatever your response to planning, here are a few simple principles to plan and execute a ministry from the very beginning.

- Identify the need and write it down.
- Share the need with about six other people and find a sense of agreement among them.
- Attempt to enlist at least three of those people to share ideas on how to meet the need.
- Engage a greater conversation with the people whom you are seeking to help. Find out what they sense to be the need and to what they would most likely respond.
- Discuss, discover, and list resources.
- Determine who will do which tasks and set a time to begin.

Dr. Wilbur W. Welch recently shared a story with me from his own life in the 1930s. While he was attending Bible college, he had a deep desire to use his newly found gift of preaching. On Sunday mornings

---

New Ministry Begins with Spiritual Discoveries

1. Discover the needs of people.

2. Discover God's will to meet the needs.

3. Listen to God through the Bible. What is it that God asks us to do (e.g., feed the poor, protect the orphans and widows, teach younger people, etc.)?

4. Listen to God through prayer. What is it that God is confirming in your heart through His Word by His Spirit? Is God continually laying on your heart a response to a particular need?

5. Listen to the people of God. What are others saying needs to be done? Are people sharing needs that no one is addressing where ministry needs to begin?

---

he just had to preach somewhere, anywhere. One Sunday morning he awoke, dressed in a suit, left his college dorm room with his Bible in hand, but had nowhere to go.

Believing God wanted him to preach somewhere, he walked out in front of the school and put his thumb out for a ride. Before long a young man driving a pickup truck stopped, offered the young Bible student a ride, and shared that their church had just lost their pastor and needed someone to preach that day. Young Wilbur preached that Sunday morning and remained in that church as the interim pastor for three months. It took personal initiative to get ready and stand alongside the road with faith and trust in God.

After this ninety-year-old saint shared this story with me, he asked a gnawing question, "Doug, is anyone doing that kind of thing today?" What a powerful question. I regret that I don't hear of that kind of initiative, but I believe it is out there. Dr. Welch's question poses a great challenge. How about taking the volunteer challenge—take the first step and trust God for the rest?

Be Introspective

Before you begin a ministry, learn to ask an important question, Does God want me to start this ministry?

Christian leadership is more about obedience to God than anything else. Life-changing decisions begin when one discovers the needs of people and discerns the will of God. God's will is best discovered by reading the Bible (listening to God), praying (listening to God's Spirit), and listening to the people of God. When these three voices speak, and you hear a unified chorus of encouragement to move forward, you will have a new confidence and courage, knowing God is at work. They are the first personal steps to know you are doing what God wants you to do. Take your time and make those three disciplines a part of your daily routine.

After the ministry is under way, keep asking the question, Is God being honored and are lives being changed? That may appear to be two questions and in some way it is. But, they must be asked together, not one without the other. Are people finding God in your ministry? Is God active and alive, doing what you cannot do? Is there joy and peace in the lives of those you are serving?

With affirming answers to the above questions, there is only one thing to do, praise God! Praise God in the ministry. Praise God with the volunteers who have invested their lives. Praise God quietly when it is just you and God in those quiet moments.

Survey Results

From question #21 in the survey (see Appendix 1):
   90% indicated they want to see the ministry grow.
   5% indicated they wanted the ministry to stay just the way it was.
   5% indicated it makes no difference if the ministry grows or remains the same.

Insight: It is long and often been said, *"Nothing grows without change."* If a ministry is to grow, it will go through change. Change will require new things. Those new things may include the ministry you start.

Question: What will it take to grow your ministry?

Chapter 10

Making It Over the Long Haul

Frequently, the difference between success and failure
is the resolve to stick to your plan long enough to win.
(David Cottrell)

You need to persevere so that when you have done the will of God,
you will receive what he has promised.
(Hebrews 10:36)

Consider it pure joy, my brothers, whenever you face trials of
many kinds, because you know that the testing of your faith
develops perseverance. Perseverance must finish its work so that
you may be mature and complete, not lacking anything.
(James 1:2-4)

But we also rejoice in our sufferings, because we know that suffering
produces perseverance; perseverance, character; and character, hope.
And hope does not disappoint us, because God has poured out his
love into our hearts by the Holy Spirit, whom he has given us.
(Romans 5:3-5)

Jesus said, "By standing firm you will gain life."
(Luke 21:19)

As I read the list of the heroes of the Bible in the eleventh chapter of Hebrews, one thing seems to stand out as a common bond among them: No one gave up. They did not quit during the horrific times, not even when they made grave mistakes by sinning against God. They were committed for the long haul. They followed God to the end of their lives.

Harvey was a volunteer in his church for nearly 80 years (he died four weeks after his 100th birthday). He did not switch from church to church or ministry to ministry. While the church he loved and served was not a perfect church (none are), Harvey knew what it meant to persevere. He volunteered for many years in a variety of roles (board chair, Sunday School teacher, etc), and he was a faithful friend and a servant of Jesus regardless of the task, role, or expectations. He was a wholehearted follower of Christ. Harvey emulated faithfulness to his family, his church, the community, and God. He never gave up.

What is most powerful about Harvey's story is that his children, grandchildren, protégé, and even his son-in-law are men and women who do not give up. I know most of them very well. They emulate perseverance. In other words, they model Harvey's life of faithfulness.

Hang in There through the Good Times.

It is amazing how many people bail out when things are going well. Right now, you might be thinking, how does that happen? First of all, successful and healthy ministries are not always growing ministries. Sometimes people don't feel needed or important if they are not solving problems or leading through change and difficult times. That is just the way some people are wired.

Some volunteers have the DNA that requires constant change and high levels of activity. If that robust energy is not present, boredom sets in, and the best start looking for something else to do. Volunteers who have a propensity to move on when there are no apparent hills to climb or mountains to conquer should attempt to develop their own internal goals with a personal victory in mind.

Finding new victories can be rewarding and enriching. While the organization may not always have clear-cut objectives for everyone

Ten Reasons Some Volunteers Quit

1. Burnout
2. Lack of encouragement (discouragement)
3. Failure
4. Unrealized objectives or outcomes
5. Frustration from a lack of training or resources
6. Negative or unkind people
7. Dying or declining organization
8. Unstable leadership
9. Lack of godly compassion and mercy
10. Serving becomes very difficult or tough

all the time, it is possible to create opportunities for growth and development. Some of them could be:

- Create value objectives for personal growth (e.g., prayer goals, building closer relationships with other volunteers, improving personal performance at your role by reading a book or finding a mentor to help you mature in your area of volunteer service, take a vision trip to visit another ministry, etc.).

- Develop some touch points for the community to celebrate what God is doing. Seek permission to bring the community together to share in praise and thanksgiving.

- Seek a new ministry opportunity that meets a need that is not already fulfilled.

- Ask God to give you the joy of mentoring another person. Look for someone who you believe is ready to learn your role in ministry. Establish and build that relationship to reproduce yourself.

Hang in There Through the Tough Times.

"I quit" can be the two life-giving words of a volunteer when the organization is in turmoil or crisis. Escape is one of the mechanisms that can easily and quickly resolve personal or corporate conflicts. Flight is a rather common response to unresolved problems from

Ten Simple Ideas to Make It For the Long Haul

1. Remain spiritually healthy.
2. Maintain close personal friendships within the ministry.
3. Learn to give joyfully and sacrificially.
4. Take an occasional break (read the next chapter).
5. Communicate!
6. Keep learning (read, try new things).
7. Remain accountable and seek out a personal mentor to encourage you.
8. Maintain a positive spirit and heart.
9. Try new and different things. Think forward; don't live in the past.
10. Encourage and honor others. (Don't worry about your own praise and rewards.)

volunteers when there may appear to be no personal loss involved, but it can have a devastating effect on the ministry.

So, how does one resist the famous two words, "I quit"? The biblical texts at the beginning of this chapter remind us of the power of perseverance and the ability to stand firm during difficult times. We need more examples of those who made it through difficult times. You can be one of them.

Here are a few thoughts to consider before moving to another ministry or giving up. Persevere by considering some of the following opportunities:

- Fervently pray for God's wisdom and spiritual counsel to discover what may be the real reasons for today's concerns, seeking possible solutions. Sometimes, just knowing the cause for certain problems is very comforting and motivating to keep moving forward.

- Be a proactive voice by sharing some positive possible directions to overcome the immediate or long-range needs.

- Communicate without being negative or complaining. Listen carefully to others and keep asking the question, "What is our mission at this time and place?"

- Offer the leadership some help. Most likely they see the same problems that you see! Be willing to be a part of the solution, not more of the problem. Offer to pray for or pray with your leaders. They will be thrilled by your overt positive actions.

> **Three Things to "Say" for the Long Haul**
>
> 1. Learn to say, "No."
> 2. Learn to say, "I have a question."
> 3. Learn to say, "Well done! Can you teach me that?"

- Be sure to share openly some of your concerns with leadership. Sometimes, leadership is not aware of the ministry struggles that you and others face from week to week. But, if they do see the same concerns you see, you will have encouraged leadership with your openness and willingness to be included in the conversation.

- Ask God if there is anything in your own personal life where you need to grow and learn to persevere during tough times.

Lee Colan in *Sticking to It: The Art of Adherence* shares three valuable multiplication factors to make it over the long haul. Colan writes: "Focus x Competence x Passion = Adherence." One without the others will not do, and two without all three are not enough. If there is an absence of any of the above, adherence is not possible. The length of ministry is a multiplying combination of all three elements. *Focus* is all about sticking to one thing and not being distracted with many things. *Competence* is the ability to do the best with what you have. *Passion* is learning to prioritize your values, with the highest value being people.

The numbers in the following two scenarios may reflect different core values related to time, energy, personnel, or abilities. Whatever they mean to you is related to your value sets. However, if no value can be assigned to focus, competence, or passion, the formula always ends with zero. So, play with this exercise to see if you can assign values to your adherence formula. It is your turn to do the math. Evaluate your factors to see where you are for the long haul.

Focus (2) x Competence (3) x Passion (3) = an adherence factor of 18
Focus (0) x Competence (4) x Passion (4) = an adherence factor of 0

Three Reminders for Volunteers When Time are Tough

1. Prayer is not an option.
2. Bailing out…too early…is too risky.
3. Walking alone is dangerous for you and others!

Hanging in There Can Bring Spiritual Surprises.

Sometimes, God allows tough times in order to shape our personal lives or the ministry as a whole. If Christ is the head of the church, and He is, then He is in control. Since He is in control, He may have some great lessons for you or your community of Christ-followers. Learn to ask God the following questions before giving up on the ministry during difficult days:

- God, is this decline and difficult time from You?
- God, what do You want me or our community to learn?
- God, is there something we need to change and do differently?
- God, is there pride or sin in our community that we need to confront? Have we become self-sufficient or lazy? Have we gotten off our mission?

Listening to God is very important during a crisis. His word, the Bible, and His still small voice through prayer can bring powerful messages and reminders to a group of volunteers and leaders.

Once God speaks, there may be some exciting rewards and "God moments." God may be preparing your ministry through tough

Additional Keys to Long-term Ministry

- Put the needs of other people first.
- Know and love the ministry in which you serve.
- Embrace being a part of the solution and avoid being a reason for the problem.
- Always give thanks and recognition to others.

times to bring you through a refining process. His golden outcomes will be worth the time on your knees, well worth the wait. God has a way of making the best out of the worst. Learn to trust God for some amazing outcomes. Then give God praise.

Hanging In There Requires a Community.

During tough times, I need you. When my patience has run out, I need the good example, optimism, and strength of other people to carry me along. It is at the difficult crossroads that we need each other. People more experienced and those who have gained spiritual maturity are vital to the emotional and spiritual health of the community. If perseverance brings maturity, we need those who are mature to help the rest of us to persevere.

Look for someone in your ministry who has been around for a long time. Get to know him or her. Spend time asking questions to learn their passion and core values. Glean all that you can from their stories, in and out of the trenches. You will be encouraged. Then share your story with others. Now, you will encourage another.

Hanging in There Will Encourage your Spiritual and Personal Growth.

The biblical texts remind us that perseverance brings maturity, completeness, and newness of life. It is a victory to make it over the long haul, which means you have persevered through some tough times. The lessons you will learn are invaluable. No one else can teach you the same lessons that are yours in the values and trenches of ministry.

The long haul will require you to pray, trust God, and work with people. Perseverance will develop your character and the fruit of God's Spirit in your life and ministry. Spiritual gifts will be of greater value as you test them during the times they will be most needed.

The biblical heroes of the faith grew the most during their persevering moments. When they made it through the course, they were given the laurel wreath to wear and discovered inner personal ministry rewards of great value and worth. Here are some of them:

- Moses learned about God's faithfulness when the people murmured and complained.
- David learned about God's promises when others tried to take his life.
- The apostle Peter learned about faith when he stepped outside of the boat.
- Job learned about God and life when he suffered through great losses.
- Abraham had no clue where God was leading him, but he learned the powerful promises of God.

They all remained faithful. Everyone persevered. They lived to remind us how to grow during tough times.

Hanging in There Is Not Always Necessary.

This chapter has attempted to encourage you for the long haul. However, there are times when leaving your volunteer role is necessary or appropriate. Here are a number of good reasons to move on to another volunteer role, or take an extended break:

- Your passion has changed to another mission field.
- You are physically or emotional drained and need to take an undetermined leave of absence. You know you need more than a short break.
- You discover irreconcilable differences with leaders or other volunteers (and you have tried to reconcile with them).
- You are stuck in routine and cannot break out of it where you are.

However, it is always important to remember that burning your bridges is never an option. Leaving your role in ministry does not need to be a time to vent all your frustrations. If you do, they will most likely be discounted by your leaving. It is when you are committed for the long haul that your concerns and complaints are best received within the ministry. Corrective comments are best received with your willingness to make a difference and assist in overcoming problems.

A final consideration is that, maybe, the ministry program needs to discontinue, but you need to continue. I hope you noted

Ten Reasons Some Ministry Programs Need to Discontinue

1. The ministry has "run its course."
2. There is no longer a need among the people.
3. The mission need has already been served.
4. Other ministries are meeting the need in a greater way or with a broader scope.
5. The resources are no longer available.
6. Apathy and indifference have ruled the day, and it is futile to motivate others to share the passion for this ministry.
7. The organization has chosen to move in a different direction.
8. Other personal priorities are right now more important.
9. You are the only one left to carry on the ministry, and no one else is stepping up to help or give you needed relief.
10. God says, "It is time to stop."

the difference in that sentence. Ending a "ministry program" may be necessary. However, it may not be about you. You may not be the problem. The problems may lie within the specific program or somewhere in the ministry. Some programs simply run their course and it is time for them to be laid to rest. Have a memorial service for the program, not for you and your commitment to the church or organization. As a volunteer you will need to find the courage and strength to dissociate yourself from the failure or the sorrowful end of the program. Now you can relax, breathe a breath of fresh air and move on to something else that God has for you.

Coretta King, the great Martin Luther King's widow, finished strong in ministry and in life. She was known for following core values as a faithful volunteer. She was courageous, focused, persevering, and unwavering in her beliefs. Mrs. King was true to herself and defined her own role in leadership. She was visible when she needed to be and spoke up when it mattered the most. She would do the menial tasks and never complain (adapted from "First Lady" by Vern Smith[1]).

---

[1] Vern E. Smith. "First Lady for Coretta Scott King, A Royal Farewell," *The Crisis* (Mar/April 2006). http:// findarticles.com/p/articles/mi_qa4081/is_200603/ai_n17184455/

Finish well! Many will be glad you did. God will be glorified and respond with, "Well done."

> As you know, we consider blessed those who have persevered.
> You have heard of Job's perseverance and have seen
> what the Lord finally brought about.
> The Lord is full of compassion and mercy.
> *(James 5:11)*

Survey Results

In the second part of question #14 in the survey (see Appendix 1), volunteers were asked to list three important core values. Of the volunteers surveyed 24 percent did not respond to this question (some indicated they were not familiar with the language of "core values"). Here are the results of the 76 percent who did respond:

- "Honesty/integrity" was the obvious number one response.

- "Trust" and "mission/purpose" tied for second place.

- "Love," "team spirit," "commitment," "training," "respect," "passion," and "faith" were each mentioned by many.

- "Joy," "prayer," "value," "service," "safety," "kindness," "authenticity," "organization," "task-orientation," and "positive attitude" were each mentioned by at least two volunteers.

- Core values mentioned by only one volunteer included "mercy," "focus," "communications," "teachable spirit," "rules," "excellence," "courage," "hospitality," "empowerment," "leadership," "rest," and "sincerity."

Insights: Core values are the things that people desire for their children to experience and own. These values are the very principles that require our protection, investment, and personal care. For some volunteers, one of these core values may be non-negotiable for them to continue in their ministry and volunteer service. Fulfilling ministry core values can best serve the volunteer for the long haul. For example, if the ministry is experiencing some downward trends in numbers or finances, I can continue serving if there is *purpose* and *integrity* among the leaders and volunteers.

Question: What is the non-negotiable core value that must exist in your ministry for you to continue to serve?

Chapter 11

Taking a Break

Remember the Sabbath day by keeping it holy.
Six days you shall labor and do all your work,
but the seventh day is a Sabbath to the LORD your God.
On it you shall not do any work, neither you, nor your son or
daughter, nor your manservant or maidservant, nor your animals,
nor the alien within your gates. For in six days the LORD made the
heavens and the earth, the sea, and all that is in them,
but he rested on the seventh day. Therefore the LORD blessed the
Sabbath day and made it holy.
(Exodus 20:8-11)

Then he [Jesus] said to them,
"The Sabbath was made for man, not man for the Sabbath."
(Mark 2:27)

One of those days Jesus went out to a mountainside to pray,
and spent the night praying to God.
When morning came, he called his disciples to him
and chose twelve of them, whom he also designated apostles.
(Luke 6:12, 13)

About eight days after Jesus said this, he took Peter, John and James
with him and went up onto a mountain to pray.

> As he was praying, the appearance of his face changed,
> and his clothes became as bright as a flash of lightning.
> *(Luke 9:28, 29)*

> Shabbat begins with you and God.
> Say "Yes" to rest and "No" to more.

You cannot serve effectively if you are fatigued and burned out. You need rest. You cannot work all the time. Work without rest is not good or healthy stewardship of your body, time, talents, spiritual gifts, and the relationships God has given you to serve Him. You need to refuel and renew your heart and spirit. Some leaders will forget that volunteers do not have "vacation" time or a "day off" like an employee. Most leaders will keep asking for as much of your time as you will give them. Halfhearted service is not what God desires.

You know it is time for a break when you are physically exhausted. How about when you are emotionally or spiritually spent? Do you know when it is time for a break? You may need to get away for a brief period of time if you are just plain worn out and you find growing tension(s) in your ministry relationships. It may be time to unplug if you are struggling with feelings of being unappreciated or not needed. If you are finding a lack of fulfillment in ministry, it may be time for a "ministry vacation."

While I was a pastor in Michigan, Bill (not his real name) was one of our most faithful and hardworking volunteers. Bill was omnipresent. He was at every meeting without fail. His involvement was off the charts. His blood pressure was also off the charts. Bill's doctor gave him numerous warnings to slow down. Initially, he paid no attention to the wise medical counsel. It was only after a life-threatening event that Bill finally woke up and realized the church was going to survive without his never-ending volunteer service. Bill got the point.

I will never forget attending a meeting a few years later where someone asked the question, "Where is Bill?" Someone else responded, "He has taken his son on a week-long fishing trip." I was never so pleased to hear that one of our faithful volunteers was *not* at a meeting. Bill had made the right decision to take a break. His now lower blood pressure and more relaxed demeanor prove just that.

What is Shabbat?

It is more than what we have often called Sunday. Shabbat or Sabbath in the Old Testament simply means, "Don't work; cease all activity; rest." In other words, take a break. God created Sabbath for you and no one else. So, let's learn how to use Sabbath—a time of rest—a time not to work for building up the ministry. Sabbath is a gift from God. It is okay to take a break.

> **You Know It's Okay to Rest When You Discover:**
>
> - You might not be able to fix things.
> - You are most likely not the only one who cares.
> - Leadership does not come running to you for help.

Why Do You Work So Hard?

Overwork can be a driving malady for many in Christian service. Often our passion for people seduces us to think we should do more. Our desire to see lives changed makes ministry exciting, meaningful, and rewarding. It seems as if the more we do, the more we realize all that needs to be done. We are caught on a treadmill of ministry. However, no one can do it all. This is the mission of God and us along with others. While ministry is never ending, God is the supply, not just us.

> **Myths about "Doing More"**
>
> - Doing more is doing a better job.
> - I will be more fulfilled.
> - The kingdom of God will be in better shape.
> - Others will see the need to offer their help.
> - People will like me more.
> - God will be impressed; besides, He expects more.
> - I can always rest later.
> - I will never burn out.

Overwork can also be an incurable illness. Our need to make our mark outside of our regular work and everyday lives drives some of us to overachieve in ministry. For some, it is a way to find personal identity and success. This is where we must be careful that our motives are clear and God-honoring. Ministry should not be for us. It is for God and the needs of others. It is always good to ask why we are working so hard.

I cannot remember the first time I heard the word, "workaholic." I believe it has been around a lot longer than the past two centuries in one form or another. God knows our propensity to pour our lives into work and busyness. Knowing just that, God created and modeled after the six days of creation a time of rest for a reason.

How to Unplug and Disengage without Feeling Guilty

Believe that being unplugged is as important as staying plugged in. God is not legalistic about Sabbath-rest. I learned a few years ago that if I plug in my cell phone or electric shaver every night, the battery will die sooner. I can't keep those items plugged in all the time. They need to be unplugged if they are going to last longer. It is not different for us in effective volunteer service. We cannot stay plugged in all the time. It is time to learn the value of being unplugged.

I don't believe God is ever going to say, "Hurry up and do more." He wants us to be faithful with all that He has given us in gifts, time, and other resources. Some days God may ask us just to be relational and simply spend time with an individual or group of people, not necessarily working. On other days, God may ask us to be alone and do nothing.

Five Ways to Find Spiritual Refreshment as a Volunteer
(even if just for a short period of time)

1. Have a daily time with God for Bible reading, prayer, and reflection.
2. Fast during major decisions in ministry and in life.
3. Hang out with someone spiritually mature.
4. Learn to establish honest and healthy boundaries.
5. Read autobiographies and biographies of godly people and listen to music that exalts Jesus Christ.

Yes, you heard me correctly, "Do nothing" to the glory of God. Now, don't panic, I will explain what "nothing" means. Keep reading.

In ministry, we need to learn the great worth of being unplugged if we are going to make it for the long haul. My body, mind, and soul need a break. Relationally, I need a break from being around the same people week after week, and they clearly need to have a break from me. After a season of being apart, there is a desire to renew, catch up, and rebuild friendships and working relationships.

We need to remind ourselves that God applauds rest. He invented it and did a good job. Since it is God's gift to us, we do well to receive it with thanksgiving, not excuses or embarrassment. Being a wholehearted servant of Christ is about being holistic. It demands balance in our busy times and down times. It requires that we eat, exercise, and sleep. We do well to reduce the stressors, and one way to do so is to rest. Try it. Take a nap and say, "Thank you, Lord."

Are you still feeling guilty about taking time away from the ministry for a much-needed break? Remember, taking time for rest is not my idea. It is God's idea. He did include keeping Sabbath as one of the Ten Commandments. Now, you won't find a better authority for getting away than that!

What to Do When You Take a Break

The first answer that might come to mind is "nothing," but resting is not doing nothing. Your heart and mind are always engaged in something. Taking a break can be a very productive time. First of all, catch up and take care of yourself. Just like going to the doctor for a physical, you need a personal ministry check-up. You need to examine your vital signs. Some of the indications that say you need a break include:

- Fatigue (beyond just being tired)
- Irritability (You exhibit a short fuse and are overly sensitive on issues in the ministry.)
- Insecurity (striving too hard for recognition and personal identity)
- Physical symptoms that don't seem to have a good reason (See your physician and tell him or her about your schedule.)

- Apathy toward God and others (Your prayer life and devotional time is almost zero.)
- Relationship stressors (More than usual difficulties arise with the people in your life.)

When you see the need for a break, don't just go off and do nothing. Become proactive with the things that will feed your mind, body, and soul. This is not a time for "retirement" as much as a time for refueling. Put into your life tank the things that can revive your soul, enrich your life, and restore the areas of everyday living that are lacking and in great need. Here are just a few:

- Spend a long time talking with a friend about life… not the needs of the ministry.
- Say "no" to something… almost anything… it may be just what the "doctor ordered."
- Start to journal.
- Start a new book (or commit to reading through the Bible if for the first time).
- Engage in a hobby, new or old.
- Finally do the one thing you have been saying for a long time you wanted to do.
- Resign from one thing to better invest in another, reducing a few stressors.
- Go sit on a rock and write down some new boundaries (limits) so you will not get this busy again.

While the above are only suggestions (along with the inset box "Five Ways to Find…") try one or come up with your own plan to take a meaningful break. When you decide to do just that, ask someone to hold you accountable to do it and report to on your experience.

Who Else Is Reading Your Gauges?

A number of years ago I heard Pastor Bill Hybels talk about his "dashboard" with several gauges that monitored his personal health and well being. He wisely charted several of life's domains and how we need to keep an eye on each one before we "blow an engine." While it is a powerful illustration, I confess that I don't always have the best view of my own dashboard. I can be distracted by the scenery and narrowly focused on where I am going that I forget to look at those simple gauges reminding me when I am low on fuel or the engine is burning up.

I know I need to take responsibility to learn to do a better job of monitoring my own health. When I don't, I need people who care about me to offer assistance in my blind spots. I need gracious and loving people in my life who are willing to read my gauges. I need to give them permission to speak honestly into my life. While that is not pleasant, it is important.

How to Take a Personal Retreat or Time Out

To leaders in the private sector entrepreneur Bill Gates said, "Take two 'retreats' a year. Leave your office to develop long range strategies." While that is not possible for everyone, it is a good idea for some. Or, just try one personal retreat on your own. Here is a simple suggestion for that first personal retreat experience. Spend 12 or 24 hours alone. Unplug everything. Go to a favorite, inexpensive place where no one will invade your privacy. It is a time for just you and God.

Simple Principles on Fasting

- Establish a time for a fast. (Begin with a lunch or dinner hour, then set aside a ½ day or full day.)
- Refrain from food, TV, or regular routines.
- Try to be alone.
- Spend lengthy time in prayer:
  o Confessing sin and asking forgiveness
  o Praising God
  o Asking God for help
- Read lengthy passages from the Bible.

Conclude your fast with a renewed commitment to someone or an area of ministry.

(adapted from Jerry Falwell: "The Biblical Position on Fasting and Prayer")

What does one do on a personal retreat? The simple answer is: whatever you and God need to do. It could be a time dedicated for prayer and meditation. You may spend your time reading the Bible or an inspirational book. You might have a great need to get some exercise and extra sleep out of your physical exhaustion. Using your fishing pole, hiking sticks, golf clubs, or taking a long bike ride may provide some re-creation to disengage from the normal routine and to engage with God. Maybe you will want to practice fasting. Whatever you choose to do is good, as long as the only two people on the retreat are you and Jesus.

Kenneth Boa, Norman Shawchuck, and others have provided wonderful devotional tools for your time away (see the inset on ten books). Google their names or find their works on Amazon.com and enjoy their insights and inspirational thoughts.

Some Good Results after Taking a Sabbath-Rest

Again, God gave rest to us for a reason. Some of the obvious outcomes include feeling better both emotionally and physically. It is also a time to invest in your God-given gifts, talents, physical body, relationships, and all that God has supplied in your ministry toolkit. You need to take care of yourself, just as you take care of other people when you are doing ministry.

Taking a break also reinforces your faith and dependency on God. Sometimes it is easy to become so engaged in ministry we forget it is God at work in us. We become self-sufficient with our own confidence and personal assurance. When we step aside, we see how God provides in our absence, and we are reminded that ministry is about God and not about us.

Time away can also renew our ministry relationships. It has long been said, "Absence makes the heart grow fonder." Sometimes, during a ministry break, we grow to appreciate the people with whom we serve. They can also take a moment to reflect on missing us. A Sabbath-rest is a good time to pray for other volunteers, leaders, and those with whom you serve Jesus Christ.

A Sabbath-rest is a good time to make decisions. It is when you are clear headed, physically rested, and spiritually charged that you

Ten Books to Read While Renewing Your Spirit

1. Lynne M. Baab. *Sabbath Keeping: Finding Freedom in the Rhythms of Rest* (Downers Grove, Ill.: InterVarsity Press, 2005)
2. Ruth Haley Barton. *Invitation to Solitude and Silence: Experiencing God's Transforming Presence* (Downers Grove, Ill.: InterVarsity Press, 2004)
3. Kenneth Boa. *Face to Face: Praying the Scriptures for Spiritual Growth* (Grand Rapids: Zondervan, 1997)
4. Mark Buchanan. *The Rest of God: Restoring Your Soul by Restoring Sabbath* (Nashville: W Publishing Group, a Division of Thomas Nelson, Inc., 2006)
5. Bruce Demarest. *Soul Guide* (Colorado Springs: NavPress, 2003)
6. Ken Gire. *The North Face of God* (Wheaton: Tyndale Publishing, 2005)
7. Nicole Johnson. *Fresh Brewed Life* (Nashville: Thomas Nelson, 2000)
8. Shauna Niequist. *Cold Tangerines* (Grand Rapids: Zondervan, 2007)
9. Gordon T. Smith, *Courage & Calling: Embracing Your God-Given Potential* (Downers Grove, Ill.: InterVarsity Press, 1999)
10. William P. Young. *The Shack* (Los Angeles: Windblown Media, 2007)

can make good decisions. You may decide on what needs to be done next as you return to ministry. It may be that you decide to begin mentoring others and replacing yourself over the long haul. A decision might be made to move into another area of ministry. Whatever you decide, this can be the best time to make changes, additions, or transitions.

So, it is okay to take a break. Finish that project at home that has been screaming at you for completion. Read the book that has been waiting to be opened. Re-engage in your long neglected hobby or sport. Pray like you have never prayed before. Re-appropriate your time. Re-invent your life and ministry. Renew your spirit for the routine you have found boring and tiresome. That may be just what God wants you to do.

Shabbat-shalom!

> Be still, and know that I am God.
> *(Psalm 46:10)*

Come to me, all you who are weary and burdened, and I will give you rest. Take my yoke upon you and learn from me, for I am gentle and humble in heart, and you will find rest for your souls.
(Matthew 11:28, 29)

Survey Results

From question #17 in the survey (see Appendix 1):

8% indicated their ministry "regularly" provides restful retreats or getaways.

49% indicated their ministry "occasionally" provides restful retreats.

20% indicated their ministry "never" provides restful getaways.

From the same question volunteers indicated:

74% felt "appreciated" when they asked for time away.

10% felt "unnecessary" when they asked for time off.

15% felt "guilty" when they asked for time away.

Insights: Most ministries appear to show appreciation to their volunteers when personal time off is needed. However, most ministry organizations are not proactive in providing time away for the entire community of volunteers. While there may be many good reasons for not planning times for rest and renewal, there remains an apparent need to serve volunteers.

Question: If you sense the need for your community of volunteers, would you consider gathering a small group of co-laborers and asking permission to plan a retreat?

Chapter 12

Receiving Rewards

Do not withhold good from those who deserve it,
when it is in your power to act.
(Proverbs 3:27)

Praise be to the God and Father of our Lord Jesus Christ,
who has blessed us in the heavenly realms with every spiritual
blessing in Christ. For he chose us in him before the creation
of the world to be holy and blameless in his sight.
In love he predestined us to be adopted as his sons
through Jesus Christ, in accordance with his pleasure
and will—to the praise of his glorious grace, which
he has freely given us in the One he loves.

In him we have redemption through his blood, the
forgiveness of sins, in accordance with the riches of
God's grace that he lavished on us with all wisdom and
understanding. And he made known to us the mystery of
his will according to his good pleasure, which he purposed
in Christ, to be put into effect when the times will have
reached their fulfillment—to bring all things in heaven
and on earth together under one head, even Christ.

In him we were also chosen, having been predestined
according to the plan of him who works out everything in
conformity with the purpose of his will, in order that we,

who were the first to hope in Christ, might be for the praise
of his glory. And you also were included in Christ when
you heard the word of truth, the gospel of your salvation.
Having believed, you were marked in him with a seal, the
promised Holy Spirit, who is a deposit guaranteeing our
inheritance until the redemption of those who are
God's possession—to the praise of his glory.
(Ephesians 1:3-14)

Wow! Those verses should encourage every believer in Christ. Talk
about rewards. Every verse in this letter from the apostle Paul to volunteers in the ancient city of Ephesus is filled with rich and amazing
remunerations and incentives to serve Jesus Christ and His church.

At the end of the day, serving God is not about monetary reward.
You know that. It isn't even about status or honors in the form of
extra kudos or outward recognition. You have been there. It is about
laying up treasure in heaven, not on earth. Jesus said, "If you want
to be perfect, go, sell your possessions and give to the poor, and you
will have treasure in heaven. Then come, follow me" (Matt. 19:21).
Ministry is about wholeheartedly following Jesus, plain and simple.
When He called the disciples from their fishing boats, tax agency,
and other walks of life, He never promised them a meaningful position or monetary paycheck.

Some Rewards from God for Volunteers

- Deep joy
- Changed lives
- Answers to prayer
- Unity with other believers
- Strength during times of weakness
- Fulfillment from using their spiritual gifts
- Confidence that they are doing the work of God

Are paychecks and kudos for those who serve faithfully a bad thing? Absolutely not! But they are simply not what we need to serve God and others effectively. Our volunteer service is to be filled with joy and thanksgiving, gratitude and grace. That is where we begin when we look for our reward.

However, after all of the above—and you have most likely heard that your rewards are heav-enly and not earthly—there are still rewards for here and now. There are "paychecks" and dividends that need not wait until heaven. What are they? Keep reading.

Rewards from God

God Promises to Reward You Now and Later.

The text from the Bible above says that you have already been blessed. While there are treasures being laid up in heaven, there is reward here and now. God's blessings are many. Read the Ephesians chapter 1 text at the beginning of this chapter again and again. The list of what God has already done is mind-boggling. Here are a few of the things He has already given you as a follower of Jesus and volunteer in ministry even before you served others: salvation, adoption into God's forever family, the Word of God's truth, the inner dwelling of the Holy Spirit, and the list goes on.

Rewards are Given, Not Received.

You have heard the words, "It is more blessed to give than to receive." That powerful phrase is not just an old parable or proverb from ancient days. They are the very words of Jesus (Acts 20:35).

There is something good that happens inside us when we give. It is a gift from God when we are blessed givers and not just takers. I get very excited when I take the extra time to shop, wrap, and create the special moment to give a gift to my wife, Donna. I think I get more out of giving the gift than she does receiving it, and I believe my gifts have been well received. One of my life rewards is giving, because I get so much.

Unseen Gifts from God

A lot of God's gifts to volunteers here and now can never be put in a box, wrapped with paper, and presented with a bow on top. God's gifts are often deep and go to the very core of our being. God's deep gifts are incredibly meaningful and can be more memorable than a tangible gift that is placed on a shelf or hung on the wall to be forgotten days or weeks later. Take a few moments to sit back and quietly consider what God has given you.

Rewards from Others

"Good job! Well done!"

"Well done, good and faithful servant," are the biblical words we enjoy hearing. "Well done" is so much richer and more meaningful than just hearing "Thanks." Those affirming words from others give us joy, unity, and confidence to continue doing what God has called us to do. We are uplifted and encouraged. Go ahead and share those words with another volunteer. Quietly watch their response.

If you are not hearing those words from others, don't be shy to ask. Make this personal inquiry, "How do you think I am doing?" If you hear, "Well done," give God praise and be encouraged. If you don't hear those or similar words, consider what you may need to do to adjust or improve your ministry service.

"Would you keep doing what you are doing?"

Being asked to continue in your current role is a great reward. It says, "We appreciate you. You have done a great job. We don't want anyone else doing what you do." Those are valued statements to the hearer. While they may not be heard with those exact words, they can be heard in the non-verbal, ongoing continuance of permission and general acceptance. Not every leader or other volunteers will say those words to us as volunteers, at least not very often. But, don't wait for the words. Simply accept your continuing role as an affirmation in and of itself. Continuance is a great reward, here and now.

"May I learn from you?"

Having someone ask you to be their mentor or coach must be one of the highest rewards in life. It indicates that you have been more than faithful. Others have noticed you excel beyond the norm. They desire to model from the best, and they have found that in your service to others. Wow, what a kudo!

I hope you hear one of the above phrases from a leader, another volunteer, or a ministry participant. However, sometimes we need to ask for feedback. Personal evaluation may require you to ask people for their honest input. A few simple questions, from time to time, can be very helpful in your role as a volunteer. Don't ask all of the following or similar questions at one time. Find a trusted friend who has observed you in ministry and ask one of these questions:

- Are there one or two things I could do to improve my role in this ministry?
- Is there anything that I should not be doing?
- Do you think I am a good fit in this ministry role?
- Do you see me growing and improving in my service role?
- Do I have any blind spots that are offensive or bothersome to you or others?

Reward Yourself

Learn to say the following statements (when they are true) to yourself:

"I did my best!"

You know whether you did your best or not. And only you can say that with confidence. Sometimes the high expectations of others will not always be met. That is okay. We are not serving only them. Ultimately we are serving God. He does not expect us to do more than He has gifted or enabled us to do.

Rewards More than Money and Praise

- **Eternal Rewards**
  Believe and know that God is keeping the scorecard and will be faithful to you for being faithful to Him. Live with the excitement of spending eternity with the people you touch and impact directly or indirectly in ministry.

- **Internal Rewards**
  In your soul you and you alone know when you are appreciated, respected, and enjoyed by others. A challenging and God-honoring environment can be an enormous kudo to those who work or serve in horrific places of stress and strain.

  Think heavenward and inward to find the joy of volunteer ministry. You won't have to search long.

Resist buying into the lie that you are worthless. Don't even try to sabotage your God-given calling to serve Jesus and others. Believe that God has appointed and anointed you to serve where you are right now, and when you give it your best, believe that you have. The voice of insecurity usually speaks very loud and performs its demeaning work. Don't buy into that nonsense.

"I was obedient to God."

We can be encouraged and affirmed when we discover we have been obedient to God's Word and His directions for our lives. Knowing we did exactly what God wanted us to do is a huge reward. We have taken our marching orders from the God of the universe. That brings us into the center of the will of God. That is rewarding.

"God, thank You for using me to make a difference."

We can be encouraged and affirmed when we bring our ministry results to God in prayer. There is a deep inner joy and satisfaction that comes from knowing God has touched the lives of others through you. At these moments and special times with God, you need to hear no more from others. God's quiet affirmation is enough!

Reward Others

The encouragement and reward another volunteer receives might come only from you, a fellow volunteer. Leaders are busy people and can overlook the importance of encouraging volunteers. Whatever the reason for their lack of affirmative recognition, try not to fall into the same quiet disregard for your fellow servants. Be the first to say the words in some of the paragraphs above. Let them know you appreciate them and believe they have done a good job. They will be blessed by you and reminded that God has already blessed them.

Personal Gratitude

It might be a good idea to create a list of those things you appreciate about the ministry in which you serve. Sometimes it is easy to take for granted the things we appreciated early on in ministry. It is just as

Some Short, Simple Words of Affirmation You Can Share with Other Volunteers

- Good Job!
- I appreciate your faithfulness.
- I am amazed at how God is using you.
- You have been a great example to me.
- It is a wonderful joy to serve with you.
- You have impacted so many peoples' lives.
- You have encouraged me to use my spiritual gifts.
- Let me share great things others have said about you.

easy to forget the everyday blessings that surround us. In some ways, those good gifts are rewards to us. If they were blessings and a source of joy in the beginning, they can be today as well. Make a short list of the things you appreciate.

- "God, thank You for the volunteer role that I have today. Thank You for calling me here."
- "God, thank You for all the good things that have happened over the last few months."
- "God, thank You for the many wonderful people that have become my friends and personal colleagues in ministry."
- "God, thank You for all I have learned since I have been a volunteer in this place."
- "God, thank You for the resources we have to honor You, and thank You for the resources we don't have that cause us to trust You more."
- "God, thank You for the changed lives we have seen in this ministry."

That should encourage you. It just encouraged me.

Creating a Legacy

One way to find great reward is to know that what you are doing today will leave a legacy for the future in the ministry or the lives of others. Great satisfaction can be realized when I know that today's efforts and unseen labor create a building block for something greater tomorrow.

If you are serving a group of teenagers, consider what choices they will make in years to come because of your influence and example in their lives.

If you are serving children, consider what impact you are having in their early informative years.

If you are serving adults, consider what kind of an example they may be to their children because of your time and investment into their growth and maturity.

If you are serving the underserved, consider just one small difference you have made today, which they will remember and cherish for a very long time.

Look at the Big Picture

One of my favorite stories is about the three bricklayers. As a man was walking by the three men laying bricks he asked the first, "What are you doing?" The first bricklayer responded, "I am laying bricks." The second bricklayer was asked the same question. He gave this response, "I am building a wall." When the third bricklayer was asked, "What are you doing?" he answered, "I am building a cathedral to the glory of God."

Now, which bricklayer do you think had greater joy and personal reward in his work? Which worker went home with contentment, eager to return the next day? I think the answer is obvious: The one who had the big picture in mind.

Your volunteer role may be totally behind the scenes. You may perform a service today that will not be remembered or recognized tomorrow. That is okay, as long as you know you were serving the greater ministry to the glory of God.

Find out the results of the ministry at large and consider that you have been a part of it. Fran has served for years as a volunteer in the kitchen at our church. She has never complained about some of the long hours and hard work. Fran knows that the lives being changed in the ministry are connected to her washing dishes and waiting on tables. Fran gets it. Each time she humbly serves in kitchen duties, she finds great reward. By the way, she is the one with the huge smile on her face.

If a man is called to be a street sweeper,
he should sweep streets even as Michelangelo painted,
or Beethoven played music, or Shakespeare wrote poetry.
He should sweep streets so well that all the hosts of heaven
and earth will pause to say,
there lived a great street sweeper who did his job well!
(Martin Luther King, Jr.)

So, whatever you do, do it with all your heart, all your soul,
and all your mind—
Wholeheartedly—and you will find great reward!

Survey Results

In question #3 in the survey (see Appendix 1), respondents were asked to share the word that best describes the reason they serve as a volunteer in ministry. Here are a number of their responses:

- "God" (the number one answer)
- "Obedience," "need," and "calling" (mostly tied as the number two responses)
- Additional responses included the words "Joy," "Helping others," "Responsibility," "Love," "Dedication," "Praise," "Commitment," "People," and many more positive reasons.

In questions #2 and #3 in the survey, volunteers were asked to complete these two statements: "The greatest joy of serving is_____" and, "One thing that keeps me coming back to my volunteer position is_____." Here are a number of their responses:

- "Pleasing God," "the needs of people" (several people groups were listed like "youth," "children," "differently-abled individuals," and more); "watching people grow," "the joy of the Lord," "giving back," "knowing I am doing what God wants me to do," "using my spiritual gift," "growing closer to God," and many more great responses

- My favorite response was, "Giving back a zillionth of what God has given me."

From question #16 in the survey, volunteers were asked the last time they received a personal note from their leader. The responses: about 50% were recent; 25% were long ago; and 25% never received a note from a leader. However, from those who heard their leader say, "Well done," this is how it made them feel:

- "Good!" (The number one response, followed by): "Appreciated," "encouraged," "respected," "accomplished," "energized," "empowered," "excited," "trusted," "honored," "humbled," "needed," "happy," and "rewarded"
- My favorite response was a volunteer who took the time to write, "I feel like 'Well done' is a higher compliment than 'Thank you.' Hearing 'Well done' seems more meaningful and inspires me to want to volunteer for my leader again."
- Only two volunteers said, "apathetic" and "patronized."

The 12 percent of volunteers who did not answer the question were my greatest concern. I don't know the reason, but have they never heard the words, "Well done" from a ministry leader? Maybe they are in the 25% group who has never received a personal note. If they have not heard these encouraging words, please be the first to tell them "Well done" for their faithful service to Jesus and others.

Insights: There is great reward in serving as a volunteer in ministry. Volunteers have indicated two of the greatest rewards: God is pleased, and lives are changed. The other rewards that are here and now seem to be verbal acknowledgements of faithful service. That seems to be true by the responses from our random selection of volunteers. However, there are so many more ways to find joy and fulfillment in ministry. Go ahead and find another reason to serve God and others today.

Question: Who doesn't receive much encouragement? Find that person and let him or her know how valued he or she is to the ministry you share together.

A Final Chapter

Is There Something More?

Now to him who is able to do immeasurably more than all we ask
or imagine, according to his power that is at work within us,
to him be glory in the church and in Christ Jesus
throughout all generations, forever and ever! Amen.
(Ephesians 3:20, 21)

The Lord said to Solomon, "I will give you what you have not asked
for—both riches and honor—so that in your lifetime you will have
no equal among kings."
(1 Kings 3:13)

To every man there comes in his lifetime that special moment when
he is tapped on the shoulder and offered the chance to do a very
special thing. What a tragedy if that moment finds him unprepared
or unqualified for the work which would be his finest hour.
(Winston Churchill)

I celebrate that you are a volunteer, serving Jesus Christ and the
people He has brought into your life. I affirm that you have willingly
chosen to give yourself wholeheartedly to the ministry along with
the sacrifices of your time, energy, and more. I applaud you for your
unselfish devotion to this calling in your life.

However, has God called you to something more? Is there a ministry that He wants you to do that is so far outside of your box and thinking right now that you would have to sit down and grab a tank of oxygen if God were to let you in on His plan for your life? Do you know if that is what God has in mind? This chapter has a few thoughts to discover if God has something more for you.

This chapter is different from chapter 9, where we talked about taking more initiative in your current volunteer role and ministry. This chapter is designed to encourage your thoughts and prayers to go beyond your current ministry endeavor. God may have something more for you than just building and tweaking the ministry you currently serve.

This chapter is about a new role for you, not just a new ministry program for the organization. This may be a life-changing chapter. It may require an enormous amount of vision, faith, and sacrifice. Life may never be the same if God is leading *you* to something more! At this point, the caution sign comes out: "Proceed at your own risk."

Go Ahead and Dream…and Listen.

While there are no shortcuts or simple answers to discerning God's will for you right now, I believe He can give you clues and signs along your journey. Here are a few road signs to consider. Pay attention to what may be blinking in your path to alert you to God's detour or change in life's course.

- A verse of Scripture is gnawing at your heart and mind as if God were speaking through a high performance loud-speaking system to get your attention. You want to block your ears and mind from God's megaphone, but you find it impossible to avoid the voice of God.

- You are hearing subtle quiet small voices that have repeatedly been whispering the needs of people in your life, and you must respond with a responsible decision to do more.

- Trusted leaders have been giving you encouragement and counsel to step outside the box in which you have found life to be very comfortable.

- You find yourself daydreaming about what you could do in ministry rather than what you must do today. The dreams are becoming routine.

- Building your career isn't important anymore.

- You can't get out of your mind a picture of serving Jesus full time. The large screen motion picture of your life is so clear that everything seems to come together from the start to the end. Nothing else seems to appear on the "screen of life."

- You are experiencing total discontent in your current role in life. All the prayer, counsel, self-talk, and more does not seem to remove the ache of doing something different. Your former comforts of life are less comfortable today.

Tom is a very close friend of mine. I have known his family well with the highest level of respect and honor. Each member of Tom's family is a professional person, wholeheartedly dedicated to his work, family, and church.

Tom followed his career passion out of college when he entered law school. He graduated with honors and began practicing law. His legal role in life led him from an attorney firm to a nationally branded bank to a promising lucrative brokerage position. Throughout each upward move in his vocational pursuits, there was an ongoing sense

---

What Might God Have in Mind?

- Consider stepping into a part-time ministry role.
- Remain open to an entirely different area of ministry, whether paid or unpaid.
- Be willing to move to another location (international?).
- Begin serious training for a new area of ministry.
- Start a new ministry where you are (see chapter 9).
- Join someone else in a brand new ministry adventure.
- Consider an early retirement and create a new "half-time." (Read *Halftime* by Bob Buford)
- Usually, God has more than we could imagine!

We Need a Few Good Dreamers

"The Western Church has become at best an employment agency for those who like to study, and at worst a movement of managers and administrators. But it is void of dreamers and visionaries."

Erwin McManus
@ Origins and Ethos, May 2006

of inner frustration and dissatisfaction. Today, Tom would tell you that it was God, trying to get his attention, the entire time.

During this time of transition, Tom had dream after dream about serving full time in a not-for-profit ministry. He had no clue what that meant, specifically. The dreams became regular, and Tom had to talk about them. The more he dreamed, the more he talked. The more he talked to his family and friends, the more they reinforced the dreams and future reality of a major change in his life. It was always on Tom's mind.

Tom could not stand the spiritual pressure any longer. It was clear that God had something more for Tom, and after about 10 years of arm-wrestling with the Spirit of the Almighty, Tom said, "Yes" to God and picked up his cross to follow Jesus. After years of prayer, struggle, and counsel, Tom went from being an attorney and volunteer in his church to becoming a full-time seminary student and part-time pastor in a local ministry. He finally yielded his vocation, personal interests, and future to Jesus Christ, 100 percent. His wife and extended family were fully supportive and immeasurably committed to Tom and his radical decision to prepare for a full-time engagement in ministry. Less than three years later, Tom is a full-time associate minister.

Tom's story is not for everyone. In fact, it would be a travesty to the church of Jesus if every volunteer followed Tom's journey. However, my

You Are on God's Mind!

We can't outthink God. Ephesians 3:20 reminds us of that! Since we are on God's mind all the time… that means we are included in His plans. Now, that is something to think about! Wow!

friend's personal adventure in ministry serves as a reminder that God can and just might do the unusual with any one of us. God is God. We will always do well to remind each other that we are not our own, but we are bought with a price, the precious blood of Jesus Christ. God is a big thinker! That is an understatement if there ever was one.

The Wrong Time to Make a Major Transition

There are good times and not so good times to make a major career or vocational transition toward a greater commitment in ministry. Some of those not-so-good times might include:

- Running from an unresolved problem or an extremely negative situation.
- Unsettled answers to being dissatisfied with your present employment and unstable surrounding circumstances.
- Thinking that I could do so much better than the current ministry team.
- I need a job!

This is serious business. It is important that we always keep our motives pure and right. Accountability with the people who know us the best is also an important factor in decision-making. A season of prayer and time with God will flag any unhealthy reasons to make a move toward ministry. Bathe your decision in prayer with a right heart and godly people speaking loud and clear into your life.

If God is Moving You Forward, Here are a Few Healthy Steps to Consider.

I remember as a little boy we would drive every year from Holland, Michigan, to Duluth, Minnesota, to visit my grandparents and cousins. The journey in our 1955 Chevrolet was a grueling endless ride for an energetic young boy, who could not wait to go swimming and fishing at Grandpa's log cabin. It was the routine rest stops along the way that somehow shortened the trip. The restaurants and museums along Chicago's skyline, the picnic places in the Wisconsin Dells, and the motel with the swimming pool created a pleasant journey. My parents knew that my brother and I needed those stops along the way. Here are some stopping points in your spiritual journey that you will do well to include as you travel toward considering "something more."

Visit Other Ministries and People.

In other words, travel. Get moving. Don't wait for ministry to come to you. Extend yourself to opportunities and people that are there to help you grow. Network and discover other places where your dream exists. Go to that ministry place armed with a quiver full of questions and open eyes. Interview the people you meet along the way, people who are doing what you hope to do. Look for as many similar situations as you can find to gather as much knowledge as possible. You can't get too much information. It is time to look, listen, and learn.

Ask Questions.

Ask God!

I hope I have not overstated the need for prayer in ministry. If I am guilty, I will take my punishment with joy. You cannot talk with God too much during this time of wonder and inquiry. Ask God every question you can think of. Then wait for the answers.

Sample Vision Trips

- Travel to two or three ministries that model your passion and desired ministry outcomes.
- Visit with two or three people you do not know who are doing what you hope to do.
- Attend a national conference or gathering of other leaders in the area of your interest.
- Invite one or two people to meet you in a neutral setting to pray and discuss (dream about) ministry.
- Take a weeklong trip to a seminary or a Christian college with an extensive ministry library.
- Visit a quiet retreat center to pray and listen to God.

Here are a few questions for God:

- "God, would You examine my heart and motives?" (Read Psalm 139:23, 24.)
- "God, is there anything in my life that needs to be changed or eradicated for effective ministry?"
- "God, is there some direction in the Bible to help me understand more clearly Your call and will for my life in ministry?" (Read Romans 15:4.)
- "God, would You give me the passion and support that I need to take the next step?"

After asking God your questions, stop to listen for answers. Realize that God speaks into our lives through His Word, other people, and the inner promptings of His Spirit.

Ask Others.
God imparts wisdom and understanding to His people (Prov. 1:2-5). It is out of wisdom and understanding that we find discernment. Start your interpersonal inquiries with people who know you best; begin with your family and best friends. Ask personal questions. Ask if they can envision you doing something more or different in ministry. Inquire about your strengths and weaknesses. Ask people who have observed you closely to reveal any blind spots where you might need to grow. Ask them to pray for you.

After your inquiry of people who know you best, ask questions of people who have only observed you in ministry. They may be leaders or fellow volunteers. Ask what strengths they have observed as you served with them in ministry. In addition, ask them about their journey and seek to discover everything that you can from their story. Remember, this is a time to learn.

Ask Yourself. Don't forget the person who knows you best, you. Take time to slow down to take a long look in the mirror.

- Ask your history what you have learned over the years.
- Ask your heart what it is feeling.
- Ask your health to consider what it can accomplish.

- Ask your mind to see if there is more knowledge or preparation needed.
- Ask your dreams to test to see if they are real and come from God.

Set Goals.

Setting goals and making plans are activities that we can do now to make a difference in the future. It is during this phase of the transition to something more that you have time to think and consider all the options and variables for the future. Plans and goals are never infallible. However, they can be a wonderful means to an end. As you move forward, evaluate your progress and adjust your goals through your changing circumstances and other dynamic variables. With open-ended planning you will be able to move through your transition with certainty and flexibility. Your road map could look something like this:

You sense God leading you to something more >
  You pray and ask God and others for clarity and confirmation >
    You make an early decision to move forward by setting goals and making plans (Plans could include timelines; information; assessments; funding and more) >
      You evaluate and adjust some of your goals and plans >
        You continue with confidence, believing God is leading >
        You make some commitments and a decision to something more.

Without goals and plans, you may never know if God is moving you in a new direction. Allow goals and plans to be your best friends in navigating through personal change. Listen to people, God, and your own heart throughout the process. Don't be afraid to make changes and adjustments to your endeavors. A failed goal does not mean a failed mission. Each goal and plan is there to help, not hinder.

Get Ready.

You have just made a decision out of your initial plans and goals to move forward. Now, a second set of goals and objectives line the pathway of change. These new plans may include extensive interviews, reading, and ongoing dialogue with a specific ministry or several ministries. You cannot get too much information in each step of the journey. Be confident in your knowledge and skills. One aspect of getting ready may include an internship or an in-service experience. Test uncharted waters. Be confident you can navigate through the new course of life and ministry.

Take Inventory.

A wise carpenter said, "Measure twice and cut once." In ministry and in making a life-changing decision it should be no different. Check out everything at least twice and decide once. As you gather information, always ask for that "second opinion." Is there more to learn? Are you finding everything you need? Do you have a variety of people speaking into your decision with multiple viewpoints and differing experiences?

Organize your thoughts with lists or journal entries. Keep reviewing the stopping points along the way. Ask God to make everything very clear and help you through major doubts or concerns.

Create a Support System.

Some of the most creative ministry dreamers at our seminary are the church planters. They are best identified as the students walking around with glazed eyes and a constant grin as they think about their exciting and scary new adventure in starting a new church. They live with their idyllic dream throbbing their pulse and moving their feet forward, one step at a time. If left alone, they could walk over the cliff or into oncoming traffic.

Everyone in ministry needs a support system. We need people who will be there to listen, offer honest feedback, and pray. Ministry is not prescribed for "lone rangers." It requires a community of fellow pilgrims who will offer their wisdom and support. Seek people now who will take this journey with you. You don't need many, but at least a few are far more important than none. Choose people who love and know God and you best.

Decide.

Some people love to skip all of the above steps and jump right to making a decision. For others this is the most difficult step. It can become a paralyzing moment in the journey. Some could not make a life decision if their life depended on it. (That idea alone is confusing.)

One tool to assist in making a healthy decision includes establishing a picture of clear outcomes and allowing the people who know you best to hold you accountable to that picture. In other words, what do you envision at the end of this journey? What picture has God given you that allows you to see the journey with clarity so when you arrive, you know it is what God had in mind?

For some the picture may include:

- Being a youth pastor at a church.
- Becoming a trained counselor for a not-for-profit ministry.
- Serving as a part-time youth worker in an inner city program.
- Joining the pastoral staff of a local church.
- Starting a new ministry to reach a marginalized group of people in your city.
- Other: _____.

Whatever the picture looks like, illustrate it for your friends and family. Keep it in front of you as you pray, prepare, and make that final decision to move forward.

However, God may bring you through this journey and process to say, "Stay right where you are." While it was good for you to go through this experience, you may discover that you will best serve as a volunteer, doing exactly what you have done for the last several months or years. Your experience of considering "something more" may be just what you needed to know that you are already doing "something more."

On a final note, you may have needed to go through this experience to realize that God has a plan B that was not your perfect picture. Again, as we face the end of the journey it is God who directs our lives and orders our steps. As you let Him do just that, enjoy the ride and give Him praise.

Appendix 1

100 Volunteers Surveyed Said

The following survey was given to more than 100 volunteers in church and para-church ministries. The surveys were given at random to volunteers within more than 20 ministry contexts, representing more than 50 different ministries. Every survey returned was anonymous.

While this survey is not intended to be a scientific survey with highly calculated results, it provides honest, open, anecdotal information, and insights from real volunteers in real ministry contexts.

Many of the survey's results are noted at the end of each chapter. Feel free to use this survey in your own ministry. It is a wonderful way to listen to your fellow colleagues in ministry. The author and publisher give you permission to copy the questionnaire.

Volunteer Questionnaire

Instructions: Answer each question by checking the appropriate box or completing the sentence.

1. When I hear the word "volunteer" the first word I think of is

    _____

    My best memory as a volunteer was when I

    _____

2. How well do you know your spiritual gift?
    ☐ with certainty; ☐ with reservation; ☐ not at all
    The greatest joy of serving is

    _____
                                              .

3. What word best describes the reason you serve in *this* ministry?

    _____

    One thing that keeps me coming back to my volunteer position is

    _____

4. How often does your "leader" pray *with* you?
    ☐ often; ☐ occasionally; ☐ seldom; ☐ never
    When my leader prays with me or for me, I am

    _____

5. How many hours do you volunteer per week?
    ☐ less than 2; ☐ 2-3; ☐ 3-5; ☐ more than 5
    If you are gainfully employed, and if money was not an object,
    would you give up your career to volunteer full-time?
    ☐ yes; ☐ no.

6. Do you prefer volunteering ☐ alone; ☐ within a team?
    I feel most included in the ministry when

    _____

7. Can you quote the mission statement for your ministry?
    ☐ yes; ☐ in part; ☐ no clue
    The direction for the next three years of ministry is
    ☐ clear; ☐ vague; ☐ not clear at all.

8. Have you ever been given a Volunteer Job Description?
    ☐ yes; ☐ no
    Would you appreciate having a Job Description?
    ☐ yes; ☐ no; ☐ not needed

9. I learned my volunteer role
    ☐ on my own; ☐ training program; ☐ watching others.
    The best way I learn to do a task or role is by

    _____

10. As a volunteer I have ☐ spent a lot of money;
    ☐ covered minor expenses; ☐ spent nothing.
    The resources I need for my volunteer role are
    ☐ available; ☐ minimal.

11. If your leader gives you freedom to lead are you
    ☐ energized; ☐ cautious; ☐ terrified?
    Which do you prefer?
    ☐ total freedom; ☐ limited boundaries; ☐ exact rules

12. Who are the primary decision-makers in your ministry?

    _____

    When you are "micro-managed," what word describes how you
    feel?

    _____

13. What word best describes the relationship you have with your
    leader?

    _____

    What word best describes the relationship you would like to
    have with your leader?

    _____

14. What gives you courage? ☐ safety; ☐ training;
    ☐ freedom; ☐ team; ☐ counsel ☐ purpose
    What three core values are important to you as a volunteer?

    _____

15. As a volunteer how often may you be creative?
    ☐ often; ☐ occasionally; ☐ seldom; ☐ never
    What is your response to routine?
    ☐ needed; ☐ enjoyed; ☐ accepted; ☐ avoided

16. The last time I received a personal note from my leader was
    ☐ recently; ☐ long ago; ☐ never.
    When my leader says "well done" I feel

    _____

17. When I ask for time away, I am made to feel
    ☐ appreciated; ☐ unnecessary; ☐ guilty.
    The ministry provides restful retreats and getaways
    ☐ regularly; ☐ occasionally; ☐ never.

18. Knowing about the ministry's history is
    ☐ valuable; ☐ interesting; ☐ unnecessary.
    Talking about the future of the ministry is
    ☐ important; ☐ irrelevant; ☐ unnecessary.

19. When I have an opportunity to share the ministry with others,
    I feel

    _____

    When people complain about the ministry I feel

    _____

20. Would you like to spend more time with your ministry leader?
    ☐ yes; ☐ maybe; ☐ no
    Would you like your ministry leader to be involved in your life?
    ☐ yes, ☐ not really; ☐ no

21. Would you like to see your ministry
    ☐ grow; ☐ remain the same; ☐ makes no difference?
    If your ministry leader had a vision for growth, would you
    ☐ do more; ☐ do the same?

Appendix 2

Create a Volunteer Retreat or Training Program

This book can be used as an excellent resource and foundation for a volunteer training or renewal retreat. Each of the eight sessions is designed to last about 45 minutes to allow time for breaks or additional discussion or teaching. The eight-session schedule is suggested to provide an interactive discussion among participants in any of the following formats (or design your own):

- Day Retreat from 8 a.m. until 5 p.m. with a one-hour lunch break.
- Overnight Retreat:
  o Friday Night—Sessions one and two.
  o Saturday Morning—Sessions three through five.
  o Saturday Afternoon—Sessions six through eight.
- Eight Evening Sessions—one night per week.

It is recommended that participants be encouraged to read through *The Volunteer* before attending the retreat. If this book is used for the eight evening sessions, volunteer participants should be encouraged to read the chapters recommended for each session before the evening discussion.

Volunteer Training or Renewal Sessions

Begin each session with prayer and have participants read the Bible texts at the beginning of each chapter.

(The session facilitator will need to monitor the time for each period of discussion.)

Note: Not every session may be valuable in your ministry context. It may be helpful to choose a few of the sessions and form your own retreat or training program.

Session 1: What it Means to be a Servant of Jesus Christ (Introduction)

A. With group input, list on a white board or paper easel the characteristics of a servant.

B. Open discussion: Discuss the role of a servant and encourage a number of people to share how someone served them and what that experience meant to them.

C. Optional discussion: Compare the Old Testament and New Testament roles of servants.

D. List and discuss the results of God's anointing in a volunteer's life to enhance ministry.

E. Divide into small groups (three or four people in each group) to discuss the biblical metaphors of the volunteer's role in the church and have each group share three ideas for improving their service to others within the ministry and outside of the ministry. Write them on the white board or paper easel.

F. Pray over the needs and opportunities listed in E. above.

Session 2: Building Relationships with Others (Chapters 1 and 2)

A. List the qualities that you appreciate the most in a leader.

B. List and discuss a number of ways to earn respect and build trust with others.

C. Discuss the things that destroy trust with other people.

D. Discuss in small groups a number of ideas to build healthier relationships with ministry leaders.

E. Continue discussion in small groups on how to establish healthy relationships with other volunteers and share the results with the larger group.

F. As a large group share what can be done to create a strong team, working together.

Session 3: Growing from the Past and Future
(Chapters 3 and 4)

A. Invite someone who has a long history with the ministry to come in and share the ministry's background and several stories.

B. Allow a brief time for questions and answers with the special guest.

C. With a white board or paper easel, list and discuss future dreams and ideas for the ministry.

D. Have individuals share how they could envision contributing to the future of the ministry.

E. Encourage people to share current needs in their areas of ministry.

F. Break into small groups and pray for the needs that have been shared.

Session 4: Developing a Ministry Outline
(Chapter 5)

A. Read the Luke 10 passage in chapter five and discuss the expectations from Jesus for each volunteer. Encourage volunteers to share their personal insights.

B. Using the open format suggested in the chapter to create a ministry outline, have people work through one hypothetical example for a real ministry role, discussing and writing down characteristics, responsibilities, and relationships. Take time to discuss the importance of each area.

C. If volunteer participants do not have ministry outlines, encourage people to take some time during or after this session to write their own ministry outline. After discussion about their experience, conclude the session.

D. If people already have ministry outlines, have them share the strengths and weaknesses within their role and area of ministry.

E. Share and pray for vacant volunteer positions in the ministry.

Session 5: Finding Permission and Building Existing Ministries
(Chapter 6)

A. Read the story in the chapter and discuss the valuable insights and principles for a permission-based ministry.

B. Have participants gather in small groups to share where they would like to explore new ideas within their current areas of ministry. Share insights and ideas with the larger group.

C. Discuss the process to create new ideas in the current ministry.

D. Have some of the volunteers share where they were innovative in ministry.

E. Discuss any of the seven results of a permission-based ministry. (At least discuss the pathway from permission to communication under the topic of accountability.)

Session 6: Identifying Personal Growth and Giftedness (Chapters 7 and 8)

A. List and discuss the characteristics of a godly person. Discuss the impact of godly people on other participants in ministry.

B. Take a few minutes to have people write down one or two spiritual goals to grow in their relationship with God. If appropriate, ask people to volunteer to share their goal(s).

C. Encourage people to break into small groups and discuss what they believe to be their spiritual gift, area of passion, and most effective arena.

D. Discuss with the larger group what people sense to be needed resources and assistance to be more effective in ministry. Encourage participants to discuss how to appropriate those resources.

E. If time permits, have each person share his or her future ministry goals or objectives.

F. Pray for one another's effectiveness in ministry.

Session 7: Creating a New Ministry (Chapter 9)

A. Discuss how and why ministries get stuck in ruts.

B. List and discuss several potential new ministry ideas.

C. Agree as a group to work through one of the above new ideas.

D. Identify on a white board or paper easel the following:
   - Mission or target group of people to be reached
   - Volunteers needed
   - Resources needed
   - Timeline to begin and establish the ministry

- First steps after this session with a plan for initial development
E. Have the group pray about the new opportunity.

Session 8: Encouraging One Another (Chapter 10)

A. Discuss the advantages of staying in one place or area of ministry for a long time.
B. Invite someone who has done one ministry for many years to share his or her story.
C. Discuss why some people quit or leave ministry.
D. Break into small groups to discuss ways to encourage others. Share the discoveries with the entire group.
E. Briefly discuss how you know when a ministry is "over."
F. Have people share words of encouragement about others (in small or large group) and conclude with prayer for one another.